the SON Tarot

Mysticism, Meditation, and Divination for Gay Men

Christopher Butler

4880 Lower Valley Road • Atglen, PA 19310

Designed by RoS
Type set in Dauphin/Book Antiqua

ISBN: 978-0-7643-4227-1
Printed in China

DEDICATION

For Simon Miles.

With love always.

ACKNOWL

The Son Tarot has a complex history with many people contributing to its richness during the long process of its creation. First, thanks must go Schiffer Publishing, Ltd. for believing in *The Son Tarot* and doing such a fantastic job to see it in print. Thanks especially to Dinah Roseberry, my editor. Your warm sense of fun made me feel so at ease when embarking on this journey. I hope *The Son Tarot* fulfills all your expectations and more.

I began this deck on my 38th birthday, back in 2005 and my main inspirations were Patric Stillman and Lee Bursten. Lee had authored the recently published *Gay Tarot* from Lo Scarabeo and Patric had created the *Brotherhood Tarot* deck and book. These were the first commercially available Tarot decks designed specifically for gay men; and apart from relishing being able to use such decks, they inspired me to make my own unique and hopefully complementary statement. Both men gave me huge amounts of encouragement and the gift of their friendship. I owe them a great deal.

Lee, in particular, helped to shape the direction of this deck and latterly the book. He is the man responsible for teaching me that it's important for gay men to "come out," but it's also even more important that they learn to "come in" to themselves through a process of self-acceptance, emotional exploration, and spiritual awareness. Early on, Lee had agreed to write the accompanying guidebook for *The Son Tarot,* but began to see just how much of a personal journey I was on through creating the deck.

"Only you can write this book" were his words to me. These words have stayed with me and inspired me to do what I never thought I could achieve. I owe Lee a massive debt.

Special thanks must also go to the men who modeled for the deck. Thank you to Steven (Brendan), Will, Chris, John, and Daniele for making the characters on these cards come to life.

Adam McClean also deserves a very special mention for his belief in *The Son Tarot.* He publishes art Tarot editions through his Alchemy Web Bookshop imprint and the first version of *The Son Tarot* Major Arcana became no. 14 in this series. It was a privilege to work with him and see this early edition come to life.

The Aeclectic Tarot Forum introduced me to the wider Tarot community as a whole. Whilst living in London, I enjoyed being able to meet up with many London-based members of the forum plus a few others who traveled from further afield. Thanks to Kay Stopforth, my *Quantum Tarot* co-creator for her constant

ACKNOWLE

encouragement. Thanks also to Jo Garner and Sophie Nussle for inspirational readings and Tarot chat that fed back into this project in its early stages. Thanks to Emily Carding for so heartily recommending Schiffer Publishing as a prospective publisher and also to Major Tom Schick for giving *The Son Tarot* one of its first outings in his ever-popular *Tarot Lovers Calendar*.

Most of all, this deck is the product of feedback and encouragement from the amazing men I've shared the creative process with or read for along the way. Thanks especially to Roger Winstanley and Don Penrose. Your positive enthusiasm has been truly appreciated and your friendship is a treasure.

Peter Clode has opened his home to me on numerous wonderful occasions. It was through reading for so many of our mutual friends at Peter's weekend gatherings that I began to understand and have confidence in how *The Son Tarot* could touch people. For Peter – you and David are the most generous hosts and I treasure you both.

Thanks to Kevin Jackson, Chris Rishworth, Ian Waft, Nobayushi Niwa, Ivor Sexton, Graham Haining, Mark Argent and Marco Whiting (aka Shokti Lovestar). You all make me laugh, make me wonder, fill me with joy, challenge me, and make me feel a million dollars.

I'd also like to mention all the men I've met through the Edward Carpenter Community. In ECC, I really feel I've found a spiritual home, not to mention the kind of community and surrogate family I actively set out to describe in *The Son Tarot* Ten of Pentacles. I look forward to growing closer to you all. As always, the most precious thanks are reserved for my parents, Denis and Sheila Butler. Their love and support underpins everything I do. I am extremely proud of who they are, what they have achieved, and what they taught me. No man could ask for more from his parents.

For Steve Guest and Jenny King. Thank you for years of treasured friendship. You encourage me in everything I do. I love you both dearly.

Final mention must go to Yale Davies and Craig McClelland. As friends, you mean more to me than I could ever put into words. Thank you for believing in me and in this project. Thanks especially to Craig for all your help with this manuscript.

CONTENTS

CONTENTS

AUTHOR NOTE

Maybe you're a gay man opening this book and exploring these cards. Alternately, you could be a Tarot reader with a number of gay male clients. Whatever the case, this deck and book set is for you. Through its dreamlike, colorful images, *The Son Tarot* opens a door to a world where gay men can explore their relationships, friendships, sexuality, and just as importantly, their spirituality. The book is written to guide you through these images, giving you the tools to perform a variety of readings and encouraging you to forge your own ways of exploration. Written by a gay man for other gay men, this is a creation from the heart. It's a celebration of true masculinity and an invitation to experience that amazing quality enshrined within yourselves.

INTROD

A RITE OF PASSAGE

Our whole lives are about rites of passage. From the day we are born, our existence involves growth, change, and a constant procession of transformations, challenges, and journeys. Some of these are joyous occasions, some are more painful. There are even times when the pathway set before us is blocked or barred, preventing us from embarking on the journey we were meant to take.

For a gay man, there is no more potent rite of passage than coming out. In doing this, we own who we are for the first time in our lives. For some of us, this is a quick process, for others like myself, coming out was a gradual process that spread over a twelve-year period.

I first came out to a small number of friends, then to my parents. Despite this, I continued to live a double life, both in my various work places and also in my spiritual life. As a member of an Evangelical church at that time, my sexuality was at complete odds with my beliefs. It would take me until the age of thirty-eight to be fully honest with both my church and myself.

Tarot had always been one of my guilty pleasures through those years and ironically, it was the Tarot that completed my rite of passage from the confused, closeted young man I had been to the confident and fulfilled gay man I was to become. Having already illustrated one Tarot deck the previous year, the notion of creating *The Son Tarot* came to me almost out of nowhere just before my thirty-eighth birthday. To this day, I don't understand why. The idea simply appeared almost fully formed like a divine seed planted within my creative center. The first photo shoot for the deck took place on my birthday and the first image from the deck was created later that afternoon.

INTRODU

The first version of the deck would take ten months to complete and I had little or no insight as to how much the whole process would change me. Tarot images are a powerful envisioning of life's deeper realities. In creating *The Son Tarot*, I was seeking to place gay men at the center of each card image and asking what their unique experience of those realities would be. You may also say I was putting myself at the heart of each card and exploring my own reality in the process.

What I discovered was the unique joy, beauty, and richness of living life as a gay man. I learned to see my same-sex orientation as a powerful expression of my masculinity rather than living from a personal belief system laden with emasculating homophobia. The realization that I was both gay and fully male became my own personal gateway to empowered living.

This is what *The Son Tarot* really is. It's a deck where gay men can be seen living the truths of the Tarot in each and every card. Not every image portrays a uniquely gay message; after all, these are universal truths. What they do show is how men like us taste and experience those truths.

If you're picking up *The Son Tarot* as a lesbian, a straight man, or a straight woman, I hope you can still use and enjoy this deck whilst being aware that our hopes, joys, and fears as gay men are not that much different from yours. If you're a gay man holding these cards, I hope that you, like me, can step into these images and connect with all those lost or forgotten parts of yourself. In doing so, may you truly become the strong, loving, and joyful man you were always meant to be. May you learn to love the gift of your distinctive sexuality, and above all, I wish you the joy of being happy and at home in your own skin.

THE TAROT DECK

INTRODUCTION

The Tarot is a deck of 78 cards originally designed for gaming sometime around the fourteenth century but now used variously for meditation, ritual magic, or divination. For our purposes we'll concentrate on the first and last of those uses.

In one sense, the Tarot is similar to a deck of playing cards in that it has four suits plus court cards. It differs in that its suits are different from those of standard playing cards, and rather than having three court cards per suit, Tarot decks usually have four. Most decks prior to the twentieth century had un-illustrated pip cards like our modern playing cards. The suit symbols were displayed in geometric arrangements, sometimes with decorative embellishments. This changed with the arrival of Pamela Colman Smith's illustrations for the *Waite* deck, published in 1909. Smith integrated the suit symbols into illustrative scenes that depicted the basic meaning of each card. This made them both easier to interpret and more visually appealing. This is the pattern I have followed with *The Son Tarot* and it's the favored model for most modern decks.

The two most influential modern decks are the *Waite* deck and Aleister Crowley's *Thoth Tarot*, illustrated by Lady Freida Harris. Both give their own unique slant on the Minor Arcana and both were born out of the *Golden Dawn Tarot* system. (Crowley, Waite and Colman Smith had all been members of the Golden Dawn Magical Order at varying times.) Although I took my inspiration from Pamela Smith in creating fully visual scenes for the pip cards, I have chosen to base their meanings on the earlier *Golden Dawn* system of keywords. Once you understand the *Golden Dawn* Minor Arcana meanings, the *Waite* and Crowley interpretations don't seem so far removed from each other and it becomes easier to move freely from one system to another. I have created my own, all-male system of court cards but they are explained in detail later in this book.

The other fundamental difference between modern playing cards and the Tarot is the inclusion of the 22 Trumps or Major Arcana cards. The word "Arcana" means "mysteries" and the Trumps represent 22 of the deeper mysteries of life. These cards deal with some of the most fundamental and underlying factors of our existence whilst by contrast, the Minor Arcana deal with our day-to-day concerns.

In this book, we will enter the Tarot via the Major Arcana, follow through to the Minor Arcana, then meet the sixteen personality types embodied in the Court cards. Once acquainted with the cards themselves, we will look at various ways of using the cards, both for divination and meditation.

INTRODUCTION

The Major Arcana is a sequence of 22 numbered cards, beginning with 0 (zero) and culminating with number 21. Many readers see these cards as a journey, or a ladder, to fulfillment, each card portraying a higher spiritual truth than the last. Others see the archetypes they portray as being of equal significance in their own right. I'm not quite sure where I stand. Each of these cards seem to be of unique importance when you see them as part of the fabric of existence, yet there's no denying the majesty and power of the highest numbered cards, particularly the Last Judgment and the World.

I leave you to form your own conclusions as you journey through these cards yourself. The meanings are basically traditional, but you'll notice several important changes in *The Son Tarot,* such as the replacement of female figures with male equivalents, so instead of the High Priestess, you will find The Mystic. The Empress card is replaced by a figure called The Bountiful and The Lovers are represented by an all-male couple. In the final card, the traditional World dancer, usually depicted as female, sometimes depicted as a hermaphrodite is now shown very distinctly as a man.

This is not a sexist substitution. Rather, in a deck specifically for gay men, I've attempted to depict the essential feminine aspects of these characters as they would manifest through a man. This is your space to discover that being truly male can also encompass some feminine ways of knowing and perceiving the world.

As you work through these images, I encourage you to experience yourself through them. Place yourself in the card. Be the character it portrays or step into the landscape you see and take your place in what's happening. These 22 cards represent one of the most fantastic voyages you may ever take.

The Major Arcana begin as a clown sticks his head over the parapet of the world for the first time. His eye sparkles with a star showing potential and he has a heart on his cheek to denote all the love he can give. On his other cheek drips a single tear. This shows that with love comes the potential to be hurt. A butterfly symbolizes freedom, but danger lurks behind in the form of a predatory cat. The scene before him appears to make no sense whatsoever. Two flamingos bury their heads in the water. Are they feeding? Maybe they are drinking. Could it be they are simply hiding? Whatever the case, they are not what The Fool expected to see. The world at first sight is a confusing place that takes time to understand and decode.

The Fool is the archetypal symbol for new beginnings, and for most gay men, one of the most significant rites of passage we experience is coming out. This single experience is often the beginning of the rest of our lives. Having lived in secret for however long, life takes on a whole new sense of freedom and honesty as we accept and embrace our sexuality. Despite our new-found freedom, the world can appear

a bewildering place as we take our first faltering steps. We are innocent and inexperienced, not knowing the many joys that wait for us, but equally, not knowing the trials and tribulations that await us, too.

Not only must we come out, but we must also "come in." We must begin to discover the reality of who we are and where our true place is in life. The Fool isn't just a symbol for individual times in our lives. Often, our journey is a daily round of new beginnings. Just when we thought we knew who we were, new discoveries and dangers await us, revealing the world to be so much bigger than we could have ever thought.

When The Fool appears in a reading, he takes us back to the beginning. His appearance denotes you're at a starting point in your life. You may be coming out. You may be discovering your identity or you may be embarking on a new relationship. Whatever your new beginning, life will never be the same again. When The Fool appears, your world is about to expand beyond your previous expectations. Dare to risk and risk to live. Take a bold step into the unknown, but at the same time, take care. The world is a vast and awesome place that can bring you joy, liberation, and freedom. But just as the butterfly soars and flies, the cat lurks waiting to pounce. A big wide world contains dangers as well as joys. It would be silly to deny these dangers. Pain and heartbreak are as much part of living as joy and pleasure.

The Fool treads a tightrope between innocence and danger. Sometimes it's his very innocence that allows him to throw caution to the wind and take the necessary risks to find fulfillment. As a gay man, you have a special and unique place in the world. This is the beginning of the exploration.

Great things await you. There will be loves, losses, joys, and excitements; but for now, enjoy the freedom of your first steps.

What's happening in your life? What's new? It's time to search out your path for today, tomorrow, and maybe the rest of your life.

O - THE FOOL

The Magician stands between two glowing wands. Storms and lightning surge through him and the energies he channels manifest between his hands as a glowing rainbow orb. At its center are the interlocking symbols of Mars, representing the energies of male same-sex love. The Magician is a creature and spirit of the air. This can be seen from the glowing triangle on his forehead; upright and divided by a horizontal line, this is the Alchemical symbol for air. He may not be of infinite power himself but the divine energies he draws upon are boundless. This is shown by the lemniscates floating above his head. This is the mathematical symbol for infinity.

Magic is a powerful energy, but when unleashed, it can also be wild and unpredictable. The Magician is the personification of this unpredictable force. When we come face to face with him, we are shown the unpredictable nature of our own human drives, particularly our libido. This encompasses our sexual drives and energies, but the libido is something much wider. It encompasses not only our sexual drives, but also the more fundamental drive to create at all levels.

Libido and life force are fire energies, but The Magician as a spirit of the air, is a channel and conductor for those energies. We see this in nature itself. There can be no fire without air to channel it. Flames can only be fanned by the wind.

If The Fool is our first tentative steps into virgin territory, then The Magician is our first experience of the world sweeping us off our feet and catching us off guard. To enter his territory is to be in a place where anything can happen next. Can we trust him? Maybe we can, but then again, maybe we shouldn't. He is our raw energies unleashed. He is the spirit of mischief. He is the playful spirit of wildness.

If he appears in a reading, he represents the unexpected. He is excitement with a little danger thrown in. He also represents the unleashing of our emotional and sexual energies when we don't have the maturity or capacity to control them. He's the force that makes us act compulsively. He's the part of us that always gravitates towards the bad boy in

THE UNPREDICTABILITY FACTOR   WILD MAGIC   MISCHIEF

relationships or the part of us that wants to sleep around when we've devoted ourselves body and soul to a lover. Maybe we all need a bit of The Magician in us, but then again, we must constantly guard against his mischief.

I - THE MAGICIAN

The scene in this card is one of moonlight, half-light and maybes. Between two temple pillars, one black, one white, we see the figure of a man, arms outstretched and rising from dark waters. He is crowned with the three-phased moon and holds a mysterious spinning disc, emblazoned with the word TORA, a Hebrew word denoting sacred texts and divine wisdom. It's difficult to tell where his body ends and the waters begin, for the whole scene is partially obscured by a veil of interlocking light and shadow. At the foot of the card, there are hints of flowers, crystals, wheels, and spirals, yet all remains mysterious and uncertain. We are face to face with The Mystic.

In a traditional Tarot deck, this card would be the female figure of The High Priestess. Indeed, the essence of this card embodies traditionally feminine qualities, yet we as men can also embody these qualities while remaining true to our essential masculinity.

In modern monotheistic faiths, gay men have rarely been recognized as having a purposeful role in society, and have sometimes encountered great hostility. In more ancient traditions, you discover a very different picture. Gay men were often viewed as mystically bridging the gender gap and were given a special place within the spiritual life of the community.

In Native American tribes, such men were known as the Berdache. In ancient Europe, there were the Galli priests, and in Africa, you would have found the gatekeeper shamen of the Dogara tribe.

The social prejudices encountered in modern society have resulted in many gay men carrying an ingrained spiritual homophobia. Many of us, myself included, have emerged from religious doctrines that declared our sexuality evil and abhorrent. Such attitudes result in a spiritual low self-esteem that is difficult to dislodge. By contrast, many ancient tribes saw men like us possessing not only a unique role, but also unique spiritual powers. As we sit somewhere on the bridge between the genders, so too we were seen to bridge the gap between the material and the spiritual world. We were seers, healers, shamen and prophets. The time for us to reclaim this heritage and to celebrate our spiritual uniquenesses is long overdue.

As we progress into the Major Arcana, we realize that we, as gay men, are not just flesh and bone. There is a hidden, transcendent part of ourselves, too. We are body, soul, and spirit. Our spirituality is a vast and undiscovered landscape which cannot be explored through the traditional, rational ways of knowing. The realm of the spirit can only be touched through the intuitive ways of knowing and through the sixth sense.

We see The Mystic through a two-pillared gateway. One pillar is black, the other is white and both are emblazoned with two as yet separate symbols for masculinity. These columns represent complimentary opposites and The Mystic reaches out to connect them. As they meet in his touch, the two symbols of Mars can be fused together, realizing the potential we saw in The Magician card. Our unions with other men are forged not only on the physical plane; they are also unions of the spirit. To bond with a lover is to walk through this gateway into a temple space where our love serves a higher purpose and connects us to unseen realities.

When he appears in a reading, The Mystic shows that you are so much more than can be seen on the outside. Discover your spiritual dimension. It's much bigger than the physical dimension you are so well acquainted with. When this card appears, it also denotes the hidden aspects of your destiny. Have faith. The answers are all there. They just aren't ready to be uncovered yet.

II – THE MYSTIC

In a moonlit wood, we can see the figure of a green man, crowned with twelve stars, each representing the signs of the zodiac and the months of the year. He is surrounded with fruits and a white swan nestles near his breast. This is The Bountiful and he represents our connection to the Earth.

In a traditional deck, this would be The Empress card, but again, we show here that men can equally embody all the qualities inherent in this traditional figure. The Empress is a symbol of pregnancy amongst other things. As men, it is impossible for us to physically give birth to children, but there are so many ways that we give birth both figuratively and creatively throughout our lives. In the widest sense, both The Empress and The Bountiful are symbols of humanity's creative potential. As a woman gestates a child in her womb, so too can we, as men, gestate our ideas and creative inspirations and bring them to fruition. This can be through arts and crafts or through the tending of a garden to bear fruit. It can be anything you want it to be.

The star crown of The Bountiful shows us another aspect of his being. The stars represent the months of the calendar and the signs of the zodiac, connecting him profoundly with the cycles of the year. We are cyclical beings. Our bodies evolved to be in tune with the seasons and it is only in our modern post-industrial society that humanity has sought to defy these cycles. We wonder why we feel so depressed and sleepy during the winter months sometimes. Is it not because we were designed to slumber more during the long nights and short days? It is so easy to disconnect from the reality of nature, when we live in an urban sprawl. How much worse this becomes now the patterns of our working lives are dictated by modern economics with its twenty-four-seven ethos.

The Bountiful is also the Green Man of traditional pagan lore. He is the spirit of the earth and its potential for fruitfulness. The Swan is a symbol of transformation. It blossoms from an ugly brown cygnet to the most graceful and beautiful of aquatic birds. To be fruitful is also to be transformative. The flower becomes the fruit. The fruit becomes the seed and the seed becomes a new plant.

FRUITFULNESS   FERTILITY   FECUNDITY

When The Bountiful appears in a reading, he shows you your substance. You are a mystical, spiritual being, but that very spirit is housed in a vessel of earth. Take time to reconnect with your animal nature. Enjoy the touch and sensations of your body. Celebrate your senses and above all, connect to your creativity. This card is a symbol of transcendent femininity. He is the feminine within us. He is all that perceives, intuits, senses, feels, and experiences. He is form waiting to be shaped. He is a fount of richness and potential. The Bountiful has so much to give and so do you.

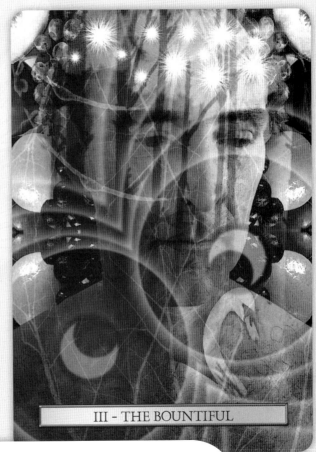

III - THE BOUNTIFUL

The Emperor sits on his throne enshrined within the element of fire. The back of the throne is shaped in the form of two great rams' heads to represent the fire sign of Aries whilst its seat is the sphere of the world. In his hand sits another sphere representing his dominion whilst above him is the emblem of the eagle, a symbol of divine rule.

This card is traditionally associated with Aries and the rams themselves symbolizes The Emperor's pioneering and adventurous spirit. If we look closely at the background, we can also see the emblem of the fleur-de-lis. This associates The Emperor with royalty and leadership.

Fire itself is a transforming element and this is part of The Emperor's essence. Whereas The Bountiful embodied all the feminine traits and qualities held within our masculine frame, The Emperor is a symbol of our raw masculine potential to shape and determine the world around us.

Seeing ourselves as wholly and adequately male has been something many gay men have struggled with. We are often reared with the unspoken assumption that our sexuality makes us less than a man; that we are somehow "effeminate" and inadequate because of our sexual orientation. We fully embody what it means to be male and manly, but sometimes we just need to be reminded.

It can help to visualize our male energy as a fire burning brightly within us. Fire can burn, but fire can also transform. As men, we all hold this inner fire. It is the power within that fuels our very being and allows us to take hold of the world around us, giving it shape and structure.

Think of The Emperor as a sculptor or a builder. He takes a raw block of stone and carves it into a meaningful shape. He takes a disparate pile of bricks and builds a house from it. This is how we, as men, take our place in the world. We give structure to meaning and potential. We create order in which others can flourish. Whenever you create or build, you are expressing this part of yourself. If the realm of The Bountiful is the field or the woodland, the realm of The Emperor is the city, the palace, or the skyscraper.

When he appears in a reading, look to your own masculine potential. If there was ever any doubt concerning your adequacy as a man, this card invites you to cast it aside. Look in a mirror, touch your body, and embrace it for all its positive qualities and also for its perceived inadequacies. Welcome to the glorious, flawed, imperfect, but very male, human race. Whatever you're building or creating, you have within you the energy as a man to see it through with confidence.

IIII - THE EMPEROR

STRUCTURE   MASCULINITY

On many levels, this is a difficult card to deal with as a gay man. The Hierophant is the archetypal spiritual leader and the guardian of traditional spiritual wisdom. He is religious orthodoxy, and for many of us, orthodoxy has been none too kind.

My own background is one of self-chosen Evangelical Christianity. I no longer follow this path, but I converted by my own choice at the age of seventeen. In hindsight, my conversion was fuelled by my own internal guilt concerning my sexuality, but I soon found this guilt increased tenfold by the anti-gay teachings and general homophobia prevalent within the Evangelical circles of the mid and late 1980s. Many of the people who hurt me were genuinely well meaning but ultimately misguided. Some of them weren't so well meaning after all.

One thing I know for certain is that this scenario isn't exclusively the preserve of certain forms of Christianity. Many of you involved in other forms of organized religion will have experienced similar negativity and prejudice. Despite this, we need this archetype in our lives. If he isn't a specific figure such as the Pope, an archbishop, a priest, a mullah, a monk, or a guru, then he is the symbolic figure of all the positive received wisdom that thousands of years of worship have brought humanity in their various forms and guises. The Hierophant represents the good teachings the world's religions can give us and we need to be careful not to throw the baby out with the bath water as we process our anger and resentment towards the various religious establishments that wronged us. It's quite a revelation to realize that you're loved by God, the Goddess, the Divine Presence, or whatever else you may name him or her. It's also a great step forward when you can acknowledge this despite the poor and misguided behavior of some of God's representatives.

The Hierophant, therefore, is the double-edged sword of religion and tradition. We have been victims of religious prejudice, but we become the poorer if we cast aside our spirituality altogether. In this card, we can see the face of The Hierophant. On the left we see his dark, negative side but on the right we can see his light, positive nature. He is also represented by an outline of Leonardo da Vinci's *Vitruvian Man.* This is a symbolic representation of the perfection of the Human form and many of us look to our spiritual leaders as some form of superhuman who will provide us with all our answers. Look closer, however, and you'll see that Vitruvian man is also filled with positive and negative.

He stands within a sacred pentagram to represent all his sacred energies. This pentagram is upright but it also contains a progression of upright and inverted

SPIRITUAL LEADERSHIP   SPIRITUAL FATHERHOOD

pentagrams ad infinitum – good and bad, light and dark, wisdom and prejudice, enlightenment and taboo. Even The Hierophant's acolytes in the foreground show the same duality. The one facing left is filled with darkness. He follows out of fear. The one on the right follows without fear for the fulfillment of his unique path. He is filled with light.

As the various symbols of the world's religions show, this is the multi-faith card of spiritual leadership and guidance. We may have benefited from our faith, but often, many gay men have also suffered at the hands of dark-minded individuals whose religious intolerance brings nothing but pain and division. We must move past this pain to move forward. Such leaders don't deserve to be followed, but if they cause us to lose our faiths completely, we are the ones who have become poorer.

When this card appears, it's time to come face to face with your spirituality. What shaped it? Who molded it? As gay men, we often have to find our own way and our own spiritual path. Maybe The Hierophant isn't a single person at all, but all those men and women who enrich us with their mysticism and guide us to a good and greater conscience.

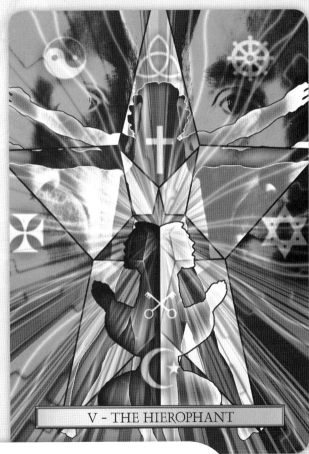

V - THE HIEROPHANT

TRADITION   WISDOM   SPIRITUAL AUTHORITY

For many of us, this card embodies our dream; to know and be known at the deepest, most intimate level by another man. This is the bond that only The Lovers know.

Despite all the desires this image evokes, it isn't an easy card, and in that, it certainly captures the reality of true love. Our Lovers are opposites – one positive, one negative. It is the law of the Universe that opposites attract, and more often than not, the most successful relationships happen when men who are wildly different yet complimentary in their natures come together and enrich each other. To thrive and grow, we need to recognize sameness in our partner. This sameness shows us we aren't alone in who we are. Another feels and acts as we do. Yet we also need difference to expand. The opposite and complimentary qualities of our partner's natures draw us up and out of ourselves, teaching us the world is a wider place than our own world views had previously allowed for. Lovers touch each other more intimately than anyone else, and when we bond with our soul mate, we bond with his similarities, finding comfort in common ground. We bond with his differences to embrace both challenge and expansion. Such a process requires maturity and humility.

One of the other aspects of this card is to show the sacred nature of our love relationships. What we see is a divine wedding, presided over by an angel or a deity. His hands are outstretched to bless the couple and also to bless and celebrate their differences. The sum of the whole will definitely be greater than the individual parts.

There is tenderness here also. Hovering above the hearts of The Lovers is a gently luminous pair of spiritual wings. The tenderness of two men bonded in love like this goes beyond explanation and certainly takes on a spiritual dimension as it grows and matures. You can't always quantify the bond between yourself and your beloved. It seems to go beyond the physical plane and stretches your very being and consciousness. Making love with such a man – the man you were meant to be with – goes beyond the physical sensations of sex to become a truly transcendent experience when both parties submit themselves body and soul to each other's lovemaking.

Tenderness and connection may be at the core of this card, but with The Lovers, we also come face to face with the power of choice and free will. To enter into union is to grow up. As we do this, we choose to embrace and accept something other than ourselves. We love unconditionally as our partner is not a mere extension of our own being. He is his own being, exerting his own free will and as such we cannot control him. We have to learn to collaborate.

A friend of mine once said that love isn't a feeling; it's a choice. The feelings we have are very much part of love and they are essential to initial attraction. When the going gets tough, however, we learn what it is to love unconditionally. We choose to love when our partner doesn't live up to our expectations. We choose to love when we support each other's mutual endeavors, even if they aren't what we would have ideally chosen. We choose to love through thick and thin. Feelings alone can't facilitate loyalty such as this. Only choice and commitment can provide the strength.

When this card appears, examine your capacity to love, examine your capacity to commit, and examine your capacity to make difficult choices in the light of commitment. Lovers support and revere each other and true love is an equal balance of interests and nurture. Are you working for each other or is only one working for the other? Choices are central here and only when a healthy balance of choices is being made can The Lovers flourish in each other.

VI - THE LOVERS

VI – THE LOVERS

This card portrays speed and momentum. A red chariot, symbolizing drive, energy, and passion is drawn swiftly by four living creatures. These have astrological significance and each represents one of the four elements. They also represent the four fixed signs of the zodiac, thereby defining the limits of the known universe. First we see the Lion (Leo), representing the element of fire. This creature symbolizes our libido, our sexual energy, and our creative drive. The Bull (Taurus) as a symbol of earth represents our physical sensations and cravings. The Man (Aquarius) is a symbol of air; an embodiment of our capacity for rational thought and reason. Finally, the Eagle (Scorpio) symbolizes water and our capacity for feeling, emotion, and empathy.

The Charioteer is the central figure of this card. He takes the reigns and brings the four beasts under control. What would, on their own, be four conflicting and wild energies are brought into a channeled unity so The Chariot can race forward to an intended destination. As the four beasts also represent the limits of the known cosmos, they show the awesome potential of the resources we as the driver of The Chariot have before us. We should never take it lightly when we take on the world. It is a great oyster with untold riches in its shell, but it's also a vast and powerful fabric of riches and energy. We are small by comparison and it's a foolish man who seeks to tame the world without humility.

We become The Charioteer whenever we seek to control the previously uncontrollable. As youths experiencing our sexuality for the first time, we discover it to be a ravening beast that can control us more easily than we can control it. Our lives and our paths to maturity involve taking the reins and learning to bring this particular beast under suitable control so it can work for the good of ourselves, the men we desire, the men we make love to, and ultimately, the men we love.

Our lives are also a study in emotional mastery. Hopefully, we gain emotional maturity as we grow older, yet discovering the art of allowing our emotions to run free within the context of healthy boundaries for ourselves and others can take a life's work. A car can only run smoothly at top speed if it's on a well-maintained road. Try driving at seventy miles per hour across an open and bumpy field and you're likely to crash. Boundaries are essential and healthy. They

THE PURSUIT OF MASTERY

channel us smoothly in the right direction.

When you learn a skill or a craft, you are taming your creative potential and channeling it towards a constructive outcome. When you regulate your diet, you are optimizing your food intake for the best nutritional aims. When you study for a qualification, you are honing your mind towards greater knowledge and enlightenment. When you say *yes* to the emotional needs of your lover, you are learning to channel your ability to give for the good of your beloved.

The Lovers have already shown us the profound and mature manifestations of Love and the ability to choose. The Chariot shows us how we attain that maturity. This card is ruled by the element of water, and water has the power to extinguish fire, shape earth, and moisten air, thereby empowering the weather. In a similar way, The Charioteer exerts his influence over the wild and seemingly untamable elements, channeling their potential and transforming them.

VII - THE CHARIOT

This isn't so much about physical strength. We see far too much emphasis on that within the gay community as a whole where physical strength, youth, and the body beautiful are given too much credence. This is the principle of inner strength. It's also about where that strength really comes from and its moral value.

There are five visual elements in this card and all are interconnected. At the base of the card we see flames. These are emanating from the base of a fiery triangle which stretches from the top to the bottom of the card. This is the archetypal symbol for fire; one of the four Alchemical triangles representing the four elements of earth, air, fire, and water. Rising from the flames and connected to them by a lemniscate (the mathematical figure of an eight symbol for infinity) is the face of a man. Finally, we see the flaming face of a lion at the top of the card. The flames of his mane fill the whole card and the Alchemical fire symbol seems to emanate from his forehead – from the place of his third eye.

The flames and the fire triangle all ultimately emanate from the Lion who is a symbol of divine might, yet these flames well up within the man at the base of the card. The message of this card is that our true inner strength is not wholly our own. We were created with a certain amount of our own inner strength but often we find ourselves drawing from outside of ourselves as a result of our beliefs or our spirituality. This card shows what happens at those times in our lives when we know we're too weak, yet the raw power to hold our own seems to flood into us from God, the Goddess, the Divine Being, Gaia, the Universe, or whoever/whatever else we believe in. We feel comforted, upheld, strengthened, and empowered. Even if you're an atheist, you will have felt the support of friends and know that their love can stoke your inner fire, strengthening it beyond the normal potential of your inner reserves.

When we draw strength from outside of ourselves, this brings with it the responsibility to use such energy for the common good. It is given to our souls with love and trust. It must be given out in a like manner.

In early decks, this card was often referred to as "Fortitude," one of the four cardinal virtues. Fortitude is inner strength with conscience. It is the ability to stand firm for what is right.

Strength is your inner fire. It is also your inner masculinity. If you ever doubted your own strength and adequacy as a man, then this card is to be meditated on. We receive our strength from the divine around us and within us. Whatever our inadequacies, real or perceived, the divine masculine flame burns within the heart and soul of every gay man, fulfilling our masculinity and making it whole. When this card appears in a reading, it points to the sheer ferocity of the fire burning within you. Treat that maleness with respect and humility. You didn't create it yourself. You were created to be a channel of it. If you feel inadequate, just remember that being a man isn't a solo journey. Someone or something is helping you to fulfill that destiny.

VIII - STRENGTH

VIII - STRENGTH

THE POWER OF THE DIVINE CHANNELED THROUGH MAN

For all our human need to connect, there are times when we must be essentially alone. Even in the closest relationship, each man will still retain a part of himself that no other human being can touch. This aspect of yourself is represented by The Hermit.

To relate, connect, and love in a healthy manner, we must first be at peace with the prospect of being alone. In this card we see The Hermit in dark and tangled woodland. Very little light penetrates this bleak landscape, yet The Hermit is not only illuminated from within, He is a gateway to a sunlit, tranquil landscape. In his hand, he holds a bright sun. In his head, we can see a six-pointed star, surrounded by the Alchemical "Seal of Solomon." This six-pointed star, akin to the Star of David, shows the union of the Alchemical triangles for fire and water, thereby representing the union of opposites.

The sun in The Hermit's hand represents enlightenment, whereas the star in his head represents him having reconciled the opposing forces within himself. His conflicts are resolved, or at least reconciled, with each other. He is comfortable, even with discomfort.

He is at peace. The Hermit is an earth card and is often associated with the earth sign of Virgo. The symbolism of the woman untouched by man is both fitting and potent; there will always be parts of ourselves remaining virginal from the touch of others. Only the Divine can reach fully into every recess of a man's heart and know its secrets.

Sex, love, intimacy, and friendship are all a yearning to connect, to know and to be known in their own ways. All these things alleviate loneliness in wonderful ways. We function at our best when we give part of ourselves to others and receive the gift of them back into our own hearts. Yet still, there must always be that inner part of ourselves that no one but the Divine can touch. It's good and healthy to seek out friends, lovers, life partners, and soul mates. But what happens if life forces aloneness on you? Even in the longest and most loving of partnerships, one man must die first, leaving the other to survive. If you're the one left behind, how will you cope?

When we find ourselves in the dark, solitary place shown on this card, this is where we must discover, explore, and embrace the reality that aloneness is an essential part of being alive, just as much as the company of others is. We can never discover who we truly are through friendships or relationships. We cannot live our lives through other men. We can only live our lives alongside them. Only when you're fully at ease with being on your own can you truly build friendships and relationships in a healthy manner.

When The Hermit appears in your readings, then maybe it's time to withdraw for a little while. There are things in your life that you can only come to terms with on your own. Others may be able to support you for a while, but when it comes to taking the steps you need to take or making the key decisions, you can only do these things yourself. When you discover the courage to be alone, then you can truly start to live. With this security within, you can give to others without the need to have your own needs met getting in the way. Never fear your own company. It can be a gateway to far more than you realized.

VIIII - THE HERMIT

SELF-DISCOVERY IN SOLITUDE

This is a fire card and when fire surges through your life, things change for good or ill. What you've built will either be purified by fire or crumble as it burns.

A secretive figure stands behind the Wheel, his eyes masked by its outer rim. As he turns the Wheel, your fate will be determined by where the arrows fall, yet the one who turns it is blind to the consequences. The Wheel is also connected to the cogs of your life. As it turns, so they also turn and your circumstances change.

The card itself is mainly purple and this color has traditionally been used to symbolize royalty or divinity. Purple dyes were always the most hard to source and the most expensive to buy, so they usually became the reserve for royal vestments. Royalty is a symbol of divine authority on Earth so the color of this card shows us that divine forces beyond our control are moving the wheels of our lives. Life may deal us good or ill fortune; whatever the case, it is in the lap of the gods.

The Wheel as a symbol also represents the concept of a cycle. What rises must also fall as the wheel completes its revolution. For frail humans like ourselves, nothing can last forever, and whichever way the wheel turns, it will inevitably lead to the same conclusion. If you are experiencing the best of life at the moment, enjoy it for all it's worth, for all good things will eventually come to an end. Similarly, if you're experiencing bad fortune, it can't and won't last forever.

The Wheel in its own way also represents the law of Karma. What goes around comes around. This can be the simple principle of our wrong actions coming back to haunt us as fortunes change, but it can also work on a much subtler level. For years, I remained bitter towards people who rejected me because of my sexuality or those who expected me to "change" myself to fit into their world view. Much of this had to do with religious repression, but I now realize just how much those experiences have fed positively into my present spirituality. Those negative experiences have helped to shape who I am. They certainly influenced the path I took in my search for spiritual reality and I know beyond doubt that I've gained unique insight through those darker experiences of life just as I've also gained from the positive. The top of the Wheel feels very good indeed – precisely because I understand what it means to be at the bottom.

Our relationships are perhaps the most important place where we must be aware of the turn of the Wheel. In love, there will be joy and conflict, closeness and distance,

CHANCE   CHANGE   GOOD FORTUNE

good times and bad. Once we understand just how natural this is, we can begin to live with realistic expectations of those around us. It doesn't always have to feel good to be true love. Indeed, real love grows through the struggles it faces more than through the good times.

Change can feel daunting, whether it's for better or for worse. We often feel as if the gods don't care when they turn the wheel; they seem blind to the consequences we experience as they crank the handle. Change is often bewilderingly complex. Who knows what the gods are thinking? When it's too hard to fathom, it's best just to go with the flow. If this card appears for you, which prize on the Wheel are the arrows pointing towards? As the Wheel has turned, how has it shifted the cogs of your day-to-day existence? If things feel bad, expect them to get better. If they feel good, savor the moment for as long as it lasts, but always be open to embrace the next struggle when it arrives. With your friends or your lovers, this is the only way you can grow.

X - WHEEL OF FORTUNE

Justice is a universal principle that we all understand. To seek Justice is to seek what is right and fair for all. Looking at the card, we see the form of a man emerging from a pillar which symbolizes truth. The Sun shines from the very center of this pillar to show that light and truth go hand in hand. The Sun is the center of the Solar System and likewise, truth resides at the center of reality.

The figure of Justice is shown here as a set of living scales. Balanced in the scales are the symbols of the four elements to show that harmony and wholeness lie in elemental equilibrium. Behind the man of Justice, we can see the sword of Justice manifested fourfold, one aspect for each of the elements. These swords are the pillars that hold up our worlds but they also rest on the spheres of our worlds. Justice is nothing if it doesn't relate to how we lead our everyday lives.

For most, if not all, gay men, Justice is inseparable from the quest to be recognized as a valid individual and the quest to be treated as an equal member of society. In my own country, the sexual act between two consenting men was only legalized in the year of my birth. In England, at the time of the writing of this book, you can enter a legally binding civil partnership as a gay man, but it cannot as yet be termed as a "marriage."

So much has been achieved in my lifetime, yet there still remains a long path to travel before true equality is achieved. Despite this, I remain privileged to live in a liberal western democracy. Even in this day and age, many countries still pass laws making acts of sex between men illegal. Some of these laws are made on the grounds of religious belief, some are made on moral grounds. How many more are passed through fear and misunderstanding, hatred, and taboo? True justice can only be achieved when the orientation of a man's sexuality is of no importance both socially and legally. It should matter just as little as the color of a man's skin.

If this card appears in your reading, it's also about balance and equilibrium. When justice prevails, people not only benefit from freedom and their just desserts, they also find the freedom to thrive within

RATIONAL BALANCE   ADJUSTMENT   EQUILIBRIUM

appropriate boundaries. Within healthy constraints, justice allows for both freedom and personal wholeness. On a personal level, it also denotes inner objectivity, a sense of true integrity and an outwardly balanced way of life.

Where sexual justice is concerned, the male species cannot experience true wholeness and integration until sexual prejudice and homophobia are weighed on Justice's scales and found wanting. Heterosexuality and homosexuality are two essential parts of what it means to be male. Not all will experience both; sexuality is a continuum across which men function in a variety of ways. This aside, homophobia splits men away from an essential part of who they really are. True justice and a true realization of what it really means to be male can only be achieved when gay men and straight accept each other on equal terms. Only then can we be internally and externally balanced.

XI - JUSTICE

XI - JUSTICE

When you look at this card, you quickly realize The Hanged Man isn't what you would have expected. This isn't someone being executed. He hangs upside down by his foot and his star-filled body is suspended within a mystical doorway. A halo surrounds his head and the arc of a rainbow reaches around him. He is a radiant source of light and energy.

There are times in life when things are turned completely on their heads and this card represents that principle. Reality isn't always as it seems. In fact, the universe is often a mass of contradictions.

We, as gay men, are one of those contradictions. The male body is designed for reproduction through heterosexual communion with women. Despite this, our sexuality points back in the opposite direction to our own gender. Rather than showing us to be dysfunctional, this inversion points to a higher reality. It shows that sex is something far more than just reproduction. Sex is a vehicle for intimacy, cohesion, and bonding. Through the physical act, human beings form emotional and spiritual connections with each other, and through these connections, we discover the essential art of protecting, caring for, and nurturing one another. This is a universal principle that applies to men and women, heterosexual and homosexual. Reproduction is an important part of the picture but there is a wider truth at work too.

The Hanged Man is also a powerful symbol of surrender. There are times in life when you can do nothing but go with the flow, particularly when you can't fully understand what's going on around you. His appearance in a reading encourages you to look at your world from an altered perspective. Things don't always make the best sense when viewed upright or head on. Lateral vision or turning things on their heads can often yield unexpected answers.

Selflessness is implied here as well. By hanging upside down, The Hanged Man has made himself vulnerable to others. This vulnerability is itself symbolic of the higher truth of selfless giving; the ability we all need in order to foster healthy relationships with others.

INVERSION   SURRENDER   LIMBO

Whether upsidedown through choice or through helplessness, The Hanged Man holds his posture with calm serenity. There is no struggle; he is simply where he is and his wisdom comes from acceptance. Go with the flow and dare to view yourself and others from an unconventional point of view. You may be surprised at the insights you gain.

XII - THE HANGED MAN

Amidst crashing waves, we see the figures of two men, eyes closed as they are visited by Death – the Rider of the Pale Horse, Grim Reaper, and Bearer of the Scythe. We see their liberated spirits as a ghostly ship, setting sail towards the next phase of their existence, whatever and wherever that may be. In the New Testament, the figure of Death riding a pale horse can be found in Revelation 6:8. In Medieval and Renaissance iconography, this figure often became combined with the scythe bearing Grim Reaper and this is what we see in our card image. Death in this form is a harvester of souls, releasing them from the bounds of their earthly bodies. He is a symbol of our deepest-held fears and a character from our darkest dreams.

In earlier times, this figure would have featured much more heavily in peoples' consciousnesses. Think of the time of the black plague when death would have been a constant component in the lives of everyone. In a world without advanced medicine, life expectancies would have been far lower, and what we think of as minor ailments in this age of surgery and antibiotics, would have spelt a death sentence to our ancestors. It must also be remembered that many people would fear the Grim Reaper as not only the harbinger of Death, but also the bringer of eternal damnation.

Thankfully, our medical knowledge is now far greater and our spiritual world view is much changed from the days when this figure was viewed with such superstitious fear. Despite this, I've unapologetically retained the Grim Reaper in this card, despite a modern trend in Tarot which tends to soften or sanitize some of the more uncomfortable cards.

The Death card isn't just a symbol of physical death, and in a Tarot reading, it should never be taken to predict such matters. It's a much wider symbol of change, decay, transformation, and mortality. Its basic lesson shows us that nothing can last forever and everything and everyone changes as time passes. For us, as men, this means our lives are finite, but it also means that our bodies cannot remain the same – nor can our hearts, our minds, and our souls. To change and to transform are a part of our existence. We cannot hold on to any one state of our lives forever.

This is why I retain the Grim Reaper in the card. He's here because we fear him, and as such, he symbolizes

ALL THINGS MUST COME TO AN END

the deep-seated fear many gay men have with regards to ageing and their physical appearance. When this card appears in your reading, ask yourself what aspect of change do you fear the most? For some, this will be the fear of physical ageing and the realization that their youthful beauty is short lived. For others, it may be the fear of regrets and the vain attempt to recapture wasted years. For many more, it may be the simple fear of growing up, leaving youth behind, and performing the inevitable rites of passage that take us from youth to young man, then on to middle and old age. Most deeply rooted of all, many of us still fear death and refuse to see it as a natural part of our existence.

When you draw this card it points towards changes of an irreversible nature. Maybe the change itself isn't the most important issue for you. What matters most is how courageously you can face it.

XIII - DEATH

XIII - DEATH

This is the second card in the Major Arcana to deal with the theme of balance. The first was Justice, and in that card, we saw the rational mind in balance. Here we are dealing with the heart.

A man glowing gold with inner fire stands waist deep in water. His forehead is crowned with the symbol of the sun and across his chest is emblazoned the unbroken upright triangle; symbol of the element of fire. The man holds two cups in his hands; he constantly pours a flowing rainbow backwards and forwards between them.

Temperance is the principle of moderation as applied to the heart, the soul, and the instincts. We see this symbolically through the tempering effect of opposing elements in the card image itself. Fire meets water and one brings balance and moderation to the other. The Sun and fire symbols show that the man is fueled by his instincts and his libido, yet his base chakra and his genitals are submerged beneath the water. Fire is tamed and subdued where it is most likely to get out of control.

The cups show Temperance to be an act of will on the part of the individual. The rainbow represents wholeness but here in liquid form, it must be kept in dynamic flow and balance. To maintain this balance, the man must continually pour it backwards and forwards from one cup to another to avoid stagnation.

Temperance isn't total abstinence, nor is it a denial of the passions. It is the passions under discreet restraint so that they may be kept in balance. In this way, we can enjoy their full benefit without them ruling our lives. Drives, cravings, and instincts left unchecked begin to rule us, sometimes becoming addictions or compulsions. Practicing the art of Temperance allows us to live in harmony with our instincts and remain in balance. In the realm of sex, the fires of our urges are tempered and given a conscience by the cooling waters of our feeling being. When sex becomes a purely fire-driven activity with no emotional context, it loses its true meaning.

On an interpersonal level, Temperance is the meeting of opposites in balance. It denotes a healthy love relationship or friendship where complimentary opposites keep each other in check and where there is a

XIIII - TEMPERANCE

healthy exchange and flow of love, affirmation, and ideas.

When this card appears in your reading, look to what your heart needs to restore its equilibrium and be open to the input of others. Both inner balance and balance with others are essential. Make sure there is a healthy flow of emotional give and take between yourself and those around you.

We see the face of the Devil imprisoned within an inverted pentagram, surrounded by images of fear and anguish. Foisted over this prison is a second inverted pentagram, but this one is made from chains. Look closely at the top left hand side of the image, and amid the chaos, you'll see an inscription which says,

"I HATE MYSELF ALMOST AS MUCH AS I HATE YOU."

In several religions, the Devil is the personifcation of evil itself. His only mission is to deceive and entrap, preventing the unwary from touching the Divine and reaching Heaven. Many of us may no longer believe in a "personal" Devil, but he remains a potent and relevant symbol, particularly in the Tarot.

The Devil symbolizes the dark side within all of us. In drawing this card, we come face to face with our inner shadow and are challenged to confront it. Fear, bitterness, anger, resentment, hatred, jealousy, and many other weaknesses are contained within this archetype. All these things have the capacity to tie us up in chains of our own making and prevent us from becoming the people we were truly meant to be.

Wherever there's an inability to reconcile with others, there's often an inability to be reconciled with yourself as well. Self-hatred plays a large part in the dynamic of this card, hence the inscription. Whenever hatred rules someone's heart and it's directed outwards, it's never very long before that very same hatred starts to seep inwards as well. Hatred and resentment become a destructive cycle that prevents us from moving forward.

What holds you in chains? What do you fear to face? Unresolved conflicts from our past not only leave a bitter taste, they often begin to seep into other areas of our lives without us noticing, contaminating our behavior and attitudes towards others in subtle ways. It only takes one person to damage our trust but how many potential relationships then suffer from our fear of making ourselves vulnerable again?

The appearance of the Devil card in a reading challenges both our behavior and our perceptions of ourselves. This is a call to name our symbolic chains and ask what negative attitudes and behaviors are

ENTRAPMENT CONSTRICTION

XV - THE DEVIL

keeping us trapped in unhealthy ways of relating.

This is an uncomfortable card. Facing your fears is a formidable challenge but the consequences of not doing so are ultimately much worse.

SELF-HATRED   FEAR

An ancient tower is struck by lightning and fire from the heavens. As it collapses, men fall from its battlements and a dove, once imprisoned, now flies free. The sky is red with fire and the eye of God watches as this once proud and strong building crumbles and falls. This card is closely connected to Mars, the bringer of War. Indeed, the lightning strike itself is shaped like the symbol for Mars. The Tower is both a prison and a defense and it is the energy or Mars that we see in conflict with these high walls.

This card represents all the false constructs we build in our lives. On a straightforward level, it can symbolize catastrophic change, but for the most part it indicates the high battlements we build around ourselves to shield us from reality. Such constructs are ultimately unsustainable and the higher we build, the more likely they are to collapse.

Alternately, if we look at the Tower as a prison; the lightning strike may be catastrophic, but it ultimately brings us liberation. Some people come out as gay men at a time of their own choosing. For others, the issue may have been forced by circumstances. When this happens, it feels like your world and your safety are collapsing. Suddenly, you're in unknown and vulnerable territory. The dove has flown free from the prison, but you're left with the question of whether you wanted to escape in the first place. Liberation in itself is a new challenge to be faced.

The Tower, as a symbol, shows us that nothing in life can be certain. Even the highest, strongest, and greatest of buildings can be made to fall. However strong we build our personal defenses to shield us from reality, we will always find the universe can send a stronger force to strip them away. Sometimes we need this to happen. It seems like cruel medicine, but it's often the choice between living a lie or living the truth in fulfillment.

When this card appears in your readings, expect to be challenged and expect your life and values to be shaken to the core. The Tower usually denotes major and dramatic disruption in your life. For the most part, this is sudden and unexpected. How will you cope? Look to your deepest-held hopes and your strongest fears. How do these affect your life? Do they rule your

XVI - TOWER OF DESTRUCTION

actions for better or for worse? What would you do if hope was stripped away and you were forced to face your fears?

The Tower of Destruction challenges us to face what we fear to face. If you've locked yourself in a prison cell for protection then maybe it's time to come out and face the world. Alternately, if the lightning strikes and deals you a cruel blow, then your challenge is to draw on your deepest reserves to survive and adapt. Life can be rich, but life can also be cruel. In the cruelest of times it's essential to know that the darkness never lasts forever.

In purple twilight, a man stands with his arms outstretched. Water flows from his hands in abundance, swelling the great river he stands in the midst of. Set in the heavens above him is a single radiant star.

In this card, we see the figure of Aquarius, the water bearer, for this is the astrological sign traditionally associated with The Star card. In Greek mythology, it was Aquarius who poured out the waters causing the great flood. In our modern times, we talk of the dawning of the next astrological "Age of Aquarius," and with that, we envisage a new era of hope and enlightenment amongst other things.

The constellation of Aquarius is also associated with Ganymede, the young man who Zeus fell in love with. Zeus disguised himself as an eagle and bore Ganymede away to Mount Olympus so that he might become the cup bearer to the gods. Meanwhile, Tros, the father of Ganymede grieved for the loss of his son. Zeus looked upon him with compassion and gave him the gift of two immortal horses. He also pledged to make Ganymede immortal, setting him

among the stars, hence his association with this card. The story of this card is one of love, transformation, and great gifts given through romantic infatuation. Water brings both life and refreshment and here we see it in abundance.

The star itself is traditionally a symbol of hopes and wishes. When you see the symbol of Ganymede crowned by the Star of Hope, the message of the card tells us to aim high and put faith in our wishes, however mighty or beyond our reach they may seem to be.

This is also a card of faith and guidance. In the Bible we read that the Magi were guided to the crib of the baby Jesus by a bright star in the heavens. When all seems dark and life is chaotic and confused, The Star talks of a clear light to guide you home. Sometimes finding our way through difficult circumstances passes beyond reason and we must simply trust in divine guidance.

When this card appears, re-affirm your hopes, your desires, and your wishes. This is a promise of guidance

OUR HOPES   OUR WISHES   OUR ASPIRATIONS

through dark times and a talisman of wonderful things to come. This applies especially to matters of the heart. The myth behind this card is of a god who moved heaven and earth for the love of a mortal man. Dream high, for someone may just move heaven and earth for you, too.

XVII - THE STAR

This is the card of the subconscious and all that stirs beneath its waters. In the card, it is shown as a lake in the dark of night. At its far shore, we see two towers with the full moon rising between them. As the moon rises, all manner of apparitions rise out of the lake.

The full moon has a mysterious and elusive effect on the animal kingdom, including ourselves. Its influence on our planet is substantial. The Moon's gravitational pull causes the ebb and flow of the tides as it orbits around us. Little wonder, therefore, that we feel its force in so many strange ways. Our bodies are ninety percent water so surely we cannot be immune to its power. On a spiritual and psychic level, the Moon has long been linked with subconscious awakening. Under its influence, our deepest instincts, powers, and desires begin to stir, and we learn that like an iceberg, nine tenths of our psyche lies hidden beneath the surface.

The first thing we see emerging from the waters is a crab. This is the heart of our subconscious and as the moon rises, it staggers out of the waters on a quest to follow its path between the two towers which mark the boundary between the conscious and the unconscious. We also see hands reaching out from the waters. These represent our needs and instincts – those very drives that ensure our survival. Dogs seem to walk on the waters themselves. Howling at the moon, these represent the emergence of our fears and insecurities.

Central to all of this, we see two glowing and interlocked masculinity symbols emerging. This is our deepest urge to connect with another man and the fount of our sexuality. The moon holds a mysterious link to human sexuality. The link is obvious with women, whose menstrual cycles are governed by the phases of the moon. Less obvious is the link to male sexuality, but the link remains. It is no accident that moonlight is a metaphor for romance.

Also emerging from the waters are a series of translucent pink triangles, representing our identities as gay men. These are also a symbol of the fears and vulnerabilities surrounding our identity. Their transparency shows all our hopes and fears in this area laid bare in the silvery light of the Moon. The Moon rules the realm of dreams and it is here that our fears manifest themselves to us in the language of symbol.

The Sun rules the daytime and the rational mind, but it is the night time and the realm of the moon which rule our deep hearts and instincts. In sleep and in dreams the chatter of the rational mind is stilled so that we can come face to face with the sub-surface instincts of our hearts. When this card appears, still your mind and listen to your heart. Don't fight your fears; seek to understand them. Tune into the language of your subconscious for it's here that your deepest instincts reside. We need both night and day. We also need our instincts as much as we need our rational minds. Tune into whatever stirs in the deep waters of your soul. The appearance of this card denotes an emotional or psychic awakening of deep importance within you.

XVIII - THE MOON

The Sun blazes brightly in the heavens surrounded by a halo of rainbow light. It casts its golden glow over the Earth as the Wheel of the Year and the Zodiac revolve around it. Beneath the Sun, we see a couple bathed in its warmth and light.

As the Sun rises, warmth, light, and renewal flood the Earth. Following on from the dark uncertainties of the Moon, the Sun brings both clarity and re-assurance, banishing nightmares and soothing our fears. This is one of the most joyous and positive cards in the deck and its appearance in a reading denotes a time of carefree happiness where life seems both straightforward and fulfilling. For the couple on the card, the warmth of the Sun brings harmony to their relationship. Its light bathes every part of their bodies, minds, hearts, and souls bringing transparency, and where there is transparency, we also find honesty.

In the natural world, the Sun is ultimately the source of all life. Not only does its energy fuel organic growth, it also fuels our weather systems. Plants depend on its light to photosynthesize, continually replenishing the atmosphere with oxygen and cleansing it of carbon dioxide. With no Sun, life would cease to exist on this planet. It is the largest single object in our Solar System; something so big and something so fundamental to our existence. Its appearance on the cards should make us look at the fundamentals in our own lives. Ask yourself: What really matters and what is truly essential? Let the Sun shine light on your own personal circumstances so that you can begin to tell the difference between the fundamentals and the non-essentials for living.

When this card appears, expect a new level of clarification and understanding in your life. What you've previously struggled with begins to make sense and you can move forward with newfound confidence. On an interpersonal level, conflicts, separations, and misunderstandings begin to find resolution, giving way to newfound joy and freedom. This is the card of good news, celebration, and carefree happiness.

CAREFREE HAPPINESS JOY

XVIIII - THE SUN

INNOCENCE   GROWTH

A great angel rises in a sky full of flames. He reaches his arms out across the ocean and calls for the waters to give up their dead. Countless men are resurrected and raise their arms to the heavens as they are drawn up from the sea. This is a rising to new life, but it's also a call to account. The Last Judgment card has its roots in Christian myth, that on the last day, the dead will rise to face God and will be called to give account for their actions and their whole life.

Whether we subscribe to the Christian faith or not, the symbol of the Last Judgment still holds several powerful lessons for us all. Firstly, it's a metaphor for our spiritual awakening as gay men. Many of us go through the process of coming out. We celebrate who we are, and in the process, we mature into a stable sense of self-acceptance. Despite this, we sometimes long for more. There's a hidden, mysterious dimension to who we are that seems elusive or locked away. This is where our search for the spiritual begins, and at some stage of this quest, we each encounter the Divine in our own unique way. At this moment, we symbolically rise from the waters, just like the men on the card. Touching the Divine or the Sacred is both a resurrection and an awakening. In connecting with a higher, unseen reality, you feel alive for the first time, even if you can't explain how.

With spirituality comes responsibility and this is the second, perhaps most important lesson of this card. When we begin to submit our lives to the divine, we are not only faced with how to live our own lives to the full. We also come face to face with our calling to help others to do the same. People can't function on a sense of spiritual fulfillment alone. There must also be conscience and an outward drive to help and enrich the lives of others.

When this card appears, it celebrates your spiritual awakening but it also asks these questions: What are you doing with that amazing, unique, priceless gift that is your life? Have your actions affected the people around you for good or for ill? What is the cost of change? Are you prepared to make sacrifices for both strangers and those you love alike? This is the true cost of spirituality; this is the cost of fulfillment. Ultimately, it's the truest meaning of love and compassion.

XX - LAST JUDGMENT

CALL TO ACCOUNT

A man stands at the center of a crossroads with its pathways stretching north, south, east, and west. He also stands at the center of the four elements; earth, air, fire, and water. His body, filled with stars, contains the whole universe, and in his hands are two iridescent magic wands. Below him is his old world; above him is his new world, waiting to be claimed. Surrounding him is a rainbow wreath, signifying both triumph and freedom.

In this card, we reach the climax of our journey through the Major Arcana. We have also come to the most powerful and positive card in the deck. The World, in its wider sense, represents the universe and the whole of creation. It is the ultimate symbol of wholeness and completion, and when it appears in a reading, it suggests that your quest or the phase of life you are traveling through have reached their completion.

We see perfect balance in this image. The man himself is balanced perfectly on one foot as he dances and the wands he holds are of equal size and power. All four directions are balanced as are the four elements.

We have a world above and a world below and the rainbow is a perfect and complete circle with stars at its four quarter points.

The wands are especially important as they represent empowerment. This man holds the keys to the power of the elements in his hands. He has attained both mastery and maturity and wields his power with wisdom and restraint. Remember also that the wand is a phallic symbol so this man has realized the spiritual and emotional potential of his sex drive. He has learned through experience that by bonding physically with another man, in both love and passion, you are elevated into a new and transcendent dimension. He knows that real love in all its facets is so much more than feelings. It is an act of communion both with your lover and also with the gods.

When this card appears, your journey may have reached its end, but this is only the beginning. The realization of your most precious wishes can only open new and more awe-inspiring doors, leading you to a whole new level of existence. If your journey has been one of self-acceptance or self-discovery, then this

XXI - THE WORLD

is a rite of passage from the immature and self-conscious inner youth to the whole and assured man who steps beyond his own needs to love and nourish the world around him. The World is the card of completion in every sense, be it personal or circumstantial. One door may have closed, but many more are opening. You may not even have dreamed what's beyond these new and exciting portals.

COMPLETION AND FULFILLMENT

THE MINO

The Minor Arcana bring us down from creation's higher realities to the level of our everyday lives. This is a series of forty cards divided into the four suits of Pentacles, Swords, Wands, and Cups.

Each of these suits symbolizes one of the four Alchemical elements. Pentacles represent the element of Earth, Swords represent Air, Wands are for Fire, and finally, Cups take us into the realm of Water. Modern Tarot views the four elements in a humanistic way. This is definitely the case with *The Son Tarot* as the elements symbolize differing aspects of human existence, and more importantly, the different components of our physical and spiritual beings.

Each suit contains an Ace plus nine cards, numbered two through to ten. Beginning with Pentacles, this book takes each of the suits, starting with the Ace and culminating with the ten. The Court cards, although an integral part of each suit, are dealt with in their own separate section later in the book.

As with the Major Arcana, I encourage you to place yourself within each of these cards. Step into the landscape and become the protagonists. How does being there make you feel and what does each of those unique spaces remind you of in your own life? These aren't mere pictures. You'll soon discover they are mirrors of your circumstances.

The sun casts its first morning rays over a verdant landscape. Beneath the Earth, the Green Man awakes from his slumber, waiting to emerge into the light of day. The sun's rays shine through the tall trunks of the trees, and within their glow, we can see a vast pentacle holding our planet Earth at its center. We also see the divided downward triangle which is the Alchemical symbol for the element of Earth.

Pentacles are the Tarot's emblem for the element of Earth. Accordingly, the suit of pentacles deals with all things in the material realm. This may encompass financial and money matters. It also symbolizes our physical acts of work and their material results.

On another level, the suit of pentacles embodies our very physical existence. Pentacles are a metaphor for our bodies; the pentagram being a diagram of the human form, it's five points represent the head, the outstretched arms, and the legs. In this way, the suit deals with our physical health and wellbeing as well as embracing physical sensations and appetites.

In the realm of love and sex, pentacles are the physical aspect of our love unions. Here we are faced with the physical sensations of sex along with the physicality of our own bodies in union with those of our lovers.

The pentagram is a map of our bodies, but it is also a map of our five senses. The suit deals with how we perceive the world around us as well as the ways in which we connect to the world through our bodies. Pentacles, therefore, represent sight, sound, taste, smell, and touch. These are distinct from the sixth sense, embodied in the spiritual fire of Wands and the intuition, manifested in the watery suit of Cups.

The Green Man himself is both a symbol of re-birth and of the cyclical nature of the seasons. He lives for a year and is reborn the following Spring. He is a symbol of the green riches of the Earth and of the harvest the Earth provides us with. Pentacles are tied to the seasons and the cycles of the Earth so they remind us of both our animal nature and our mortality. We too are part of the great cycle of rise and fall, death and rebirth.

When this card appears in your reading, expect a new beginning in any of these areas. This is the germination of a seed as the spring rains and the

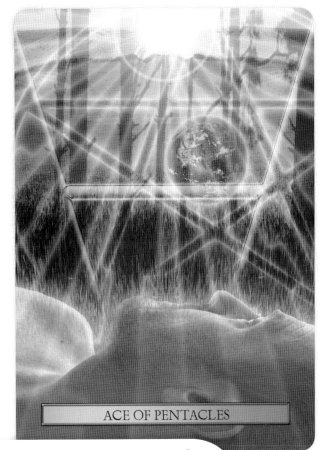

ACE OF PENTACLES

sun awaken life beneath the soil. The Ace of Pentacles brings a promise of fertility, growth, and abundance but enjoy these things in their season. Nothing lasts forever and everything rises and falls as it takes its place in the cycles of life.

Two is the number of partnership and companionship. With this number, we discover we're not alone. Partnership, companionship, love, and any other mode which allows another human being into our space will inevitably spell change on a practical level.

On the card, we see a man juggling two pentacles bound together by a ribbon of fate. The movement of one is affected by the other, whichever way they are thrown. We can also see this man's vision of his companion and how he seems to be juggling the pentacles as well. To each, the other seems to be the juggler, but the reality is they are both working to keep the pentacles in the air.

In any sort of partnership, be it a romantic, friendship, or work partnership, the everyday dynamics and the practicalities of your life change. Two men building a life together under the same roof is something very different from the everyday routine of a single person. Responsibilities are shared, finances are merged, and your day-to-day routine becomes interactive rather than solitary.

In a work partnership or collaboration, two sets of ideas are being pooled and manifested. There are twice the resources and twice the human energy being poured into the manifestation of physical wealth. In friendships, as in romantic relationships, the directions chosen are for the benefit and wellbeing of two people rather than one. In the sexual realm, essential inner change is manifested through a selfless and satisfying physical union. We learn intimate dance as we forget our own cravings and needs and focus on pleasuring our lover's body. If the dance is selfless on both parts, sex becomes deeply rewarding. The focus is all on "him," yet we are caught off guard with delicious pleasures as he also takes us by surprise, using his own selfless pre-occupation for your physical fulfillment. Learning to make love in this manner is a role model for life. True selflessness in relationships of any kind leads to a strong bond of loyalty and welfare. If this card relates to sex, it's very much about learning change through selfless giving.

Change is dynamic and constant when we choose to open our space to someone else. Like the men in the card, our lives become an act of juggling resources. Change is a dance that we only truly experience as we open ourselves to others. To change is to grow, to be enriched and to evolve.

When this card appears, allow yourself to be open to the influence of others and be open to change on a physical level. Don't cling to rigid routines, particularly if you're in a relationship. For your love to grow and thrive, it must be practical as well as romantic. Dare to trust and be brave enough to build a practical framework within which you can share your lives together.

TWO OF PENTACLES

HARMONIOUS CHANGE

𝒥𝓃 this card, the Pentacles are depicted as three large revolving cogs, each nestled within the outstretched arms of a man. These cogs interlock with each other and the movement of one will inevitably affect the movement of the others. Cogs are symbols of machinery, manufacturing, productivity, and industry. This is the card of work.

Two is the number of partnership whereas three is the number of collaboration, cooperation, and collective effort. Within the gay community, I best saw this principle modeled when I lived in London in my thirties. One of my friends lived in a very large house which he'd previously pooled resources to buy with four other friends. All of these men had been diagnosed HIV positive and sadly, by the time I met this man, he was the last surviving occupant of the once loving and bustling community.

This house was a testament to the power of friends to work together for the common good of each other. Each of these men had surrendered their financial and domestic independence in order to create a comfortable and supportive environment for each other. There had been four tragic deaths under that roof and each of these men had seen a lot of suffering, but when seen from the other side of the coin, nobody in the house had died alone. Each of these men was loved and supported with the kindness and care only those closest to him could have given. They died knowing they were loved. Even for my friend who outlived his four house mates, the financial legacy gifted to him through the house and its contents will insure that he can receive all the care and support he needs as, and when, the necessity arises.

The legacy left by these men shows the gay community has powerful ways of caring for its own. When this card appears, see it as an encouragement to channel your energies selflessly. The greatest examples of architecture are always collaborative efforts. Where can you selflessly channel your skills and physical resources for the benefit of the greatest number of people? The laws of Karma never fail, and in working selflessly with others, you'll soon find you get back tenfold what you've given.

III

MATERIAL WORKS

This is a depiction of pure physical power. Four is the number of foursquare stability. Of all the elements, Earth fits the most comfortably with this notion; Crowley's *Thoth Tarot* depicts an aerial view of a fortress with its four corners representing the pentacles on the card. This card shows rock solid stability and physical power. In stormy times, having unshakable physical and financial foundations can be a major blessing. Sound physical health is also a hallmark of this card, along with boundless sexual strength and staying power. Equally, this card is about the abuse of earthly power. A miser will cling to his earthly riches rather than see them shared. Generosity dies through an unhealthy obsession with personal security.

Body fascism can be another form of power craving for unhealthy reasons. The card shows a muscle man surrounded by a foursquare cage of pentacles. Looking on enviously is another man who craves to have the same physical appearance as our prisoner. Misplaced pride and envy are the two factors in this image. The muscle boy thinks his beauty

and physical build, often obtained through numerous hours in the gym, makes him superior and somehow more acceptable to himself and others. The onlooker thinks his lack of these attributes makes him inferior and he craves them like an all-purpose fix.

Stereotypes are dangerous and nothing could be more dangerous than the misplaced quest for superiority through "obtaining" beauty. Misers aren't powerful because they have hoards of money. They are weak because they don't see themselves as valid people unless they have riches to cling to. Similarly, you can't find peace and strength through a misplaced quest for physical perfection. Men come in all shapes and sizes and beauty doesn't conform to stereotypes. Each man you meet is beautiful in his own way. The fat guy is just as much a unique and awesome force of nature as the porn star, and to someone out there, he'll be just as much the strong, caring lover who can fulfill his heart to the very depths.

We're all beautiful. To be natural and happy with yourself the way you were made is one of the greatest affirmations you can know. When this card appears, it speaks of empowerment. Don't chase impossible stereotypes. It's more important that you understand and affirm your real potential and uniqueness.

EARTHLY POWER

Fives usually represent difficulty and instability and here we see this manifested as worry or material trouble. The man in the card is literally "out in the cold." It is night; snow falls and he stands naked outside a building whose doors are firmly closed against him. Five rainbow colored pentacles are contained within the door arch above him.

Most gay men will know what it's like to have been left out in the cold at some stage in their lives. In an extreme case, one of my friends was ostracized by his family in his teens when they discovered he was gay. Left to fend for himself, he was left homeless and without means of financial support. The kindness and support of friends allowed him to rebuild an independent life, but the emotional scars remain to this day and he has never been reconciled with his parents.

Relationship break ups and divorce inevitably lead to periods of material worry and difficulty. Men who have previously lived comfortable and prosperous lives suddenly find themselves starting again as the family or joint home is sold and divided between the separating parties. Traumas like these can take their toll on our well-being, and often, as men, we can feel we've failed or we believe nobody could have gotten it as wrong as we did.

Men often share their feelings with reluctance, but when this card appears in your readings, it's a signal to draw on your support networks. If life's throwing hell at you and you find yourself in unfamiliar and frightening territory, you can't survive on your own. Seek the comfort of friends. Seek the warm embrace and re-assurance of a lover, and if you really do find yourself totally alone, get on the Internet and seek out a suitable support organization that can advise you and provide practical help.

Having people around you doesn't often banish serious troubles like these, but it does take the sting out of their tail. In this card, the rainbow pentacles represent the support and comfort that can always be found if only you look. Gay men can be a strange bunch, but experience has taught me that despite some very insincere people, there will always be some incredibly selfless men along your path who won't see

you fall. In my life, these men have become my heroes. They know who they are and I hope they also know just how much I will always treasure their love and friendship.

In the UK, we have a name for the formidable spending power of the gay community. We call it "The Pink Pound." Gay men have traditionally had many factors stacked against them, but as western society has become progressively more liberal, a certain class of gay man has become more visible, proving that the cards are not always stacked against us. These men have all worked hard to establish themselves, but unlike their straight friends who married and started families in their twenties and thirties, they are childless and consequently in possession of financial and social freedoms unknown to their straight counterparts.

Of course, many of us won't have the consolation of grown-up children to care for us as we get older. I've recently been reminded of this as one of my best friends cared for his Father through terminal cancer. As I watched him nurse his Father, we both asked "Who will do this for us when the time comes?" There's no answer to a question like this. We can only hope and trust in the kindness and compassion of those close to us in years to come.

In the meantime, many gay men find themselves in the enviable position of being masters of their own destiny without the practical expenditure that family commitments bring. Much about this card also has to do with recognizing life's generosity to us. Hands reach out to catch glowing pentacles that fall from the hands of the gods.

If you draw this card in a reading, remember the hard times you've experienced and take stock of the prosperity you have now or may experience in the future. Wealth is a gift, not a right. You may have it in your hands but there are millions of others in the world who have very little. Enjoy every penny and pentacle of it, but never lose sight of the privileges you've been given. Take time to reflect on the freedoms and riches your sexuality has given you. You may be surprised just how wealthy you are.

A man looks wistfully across a desert at dusk. In the distance is a vision of a giant yuletide tree filling the sky. Its branches are lit by seven glowing pentacles.

When I was a child, the one day of the year I used to look forward to the most was the day when our white imitation Christmas tree would be brought down from the loft and decorated with tinsel, baubles, and glowing lights shaped like stars, carriages, and lanterns. In some ways, this was more exciting than Christmas day itself. The house took on an almost magical aura and each of those tree lights seemed to symbolize a wish, a desire, or one of the Christmas presents that would eventually sit under the tree; like a tree laden with fruit, our Christmas tree with its bright lights was laden with all my hopes.

In this card, the tree still glows with hopes and aspirations, but it seems so distant, so totally unobtainable that the man in the card can only stare at it despondently. This is the card of success unfulfilled, the card of material failure.

I didn't fully come out until my thirties. Prior to that, I'd been involved in the most unhealthy kind of evangelical Christianity and had consequently denied my sexuality. Coming out was a true liberation, but I quickly realized there were several important factors missing in my life. I truly felt as if I'd missed the boat.

Some of my gay friends had used their twenties and thirties wisely, investing time, effort, money, and sheer hard work in their relationships and their homes. Having reached their late thirties, these men were settled with long-term partners and enjoying the security of their home lives together. By contrast, I had actively avoided commitment and relationships. Having come out, I found myself alone and facing the prospect of starting from scratch as I approached forty.

Of course, this view of things was partially idealized; but the fact remains, I was looking at my own personal Christmas tree from a great distance and feeling unable to pluck those fulfilled wishes from its branches.

There's no easy answer to this card when it appears in a reading. You can stare at the tree feeling short changed by life, you can wallow in your own mistakes, or you can make the decision to go out there and make your wishes happen, however hard that may be. Success unfulfilled is not success denied. You may have a long journey ahead of you to make your dreams come true, but your destiny is indeed in your hands and you can make it happen. To do nothing is to stagnate. Pick yourself up and shake yourself down. Things may not have turned out how you wanted, but life can still deliver what you desire the most. It's in your hands and no-one else's.

VII

SEVEN OF PENTACLES

UNFULFILLED SUCCESS

Prudence is all about avoiding risks rather than taking them. In the Eight of Pentacles, we see this man's skills, talents, and visions manifest as eight glowing pentacles, each brought to life through the touch of his finger. Work and momentum are each symbolized by the presence of cogs and a speedometer respectively.

We all have talents and skills. Many of the gay men I know have turned these skills to wise use, manifesting success and wealth for themselves, either through suitable employment or their own business ventures. On the other hand, I've also seen many gay men underachieve through lack of confidence in their own masculine abilities. How many guys have you met who seem to drift through life with no clear vision or aspiration, going from one job to another? I often wonder how much this is connected to lack of acceptance. Many of us have had to fight for validation from friends, family, and society. The battle for acceptance has swallowed up valuable time and energy that would have otherwise been spent discovering our talents and potential.

Alternately, how many of you have come across the over-achieving, workaholic gay man who is so busy proving his masculine strength to the world that he finds himself with a wealthy but ultimately unfulfilling empire? I have two closeted friends who have climbed to the top of the corporate ladder. Both are rich, yet both are lonely. Work has become an obsession that shields them from their unresolved issues. They have both succeeded in a spectacular manner, yet neither has ever asked questions about whether the path they took was the right one for them.

This card is about knowing yourself, your strengths and weaknesses as a man and about making informed choices. Know your skills and talents, then make informed, unhurried choices about how best to turn your skills to material gain. For several years I worked in the rail industry. Financially I was very successful, and to a partial extent, I enjoyed my work. Despite this, it was more about proving I could be successful, having had several career failures in my teens and twenties. I earned a lot of money and

I managed to buy myself a beautiful house, but ultimately, the job left me feeling empty. I was also trying to prove to myself that I could fully compete in a traditionally "male" environment.

My ultimate career path took me somewhere very different and I no longer feel the need to prove myself in that arena. My skills are as an artist, as a writer, and as a Tarot reader. Careful planning has allowed me to slowly build my passions into a business. What's your true vocation? Be prudent and you'll find your efforts will be fruitful.

EIGHT OF PENTACLES

You know yourself. You're a confident and affirmed man. Not only do you know your gifts, your talents, your strengths, and your weaknesses, but you've also been able to turn them to the generation of material prosperity.

This is a collage of affluence as experienced on a personal level. There is fruit to suggest abundance and there are nine pentacles glowing within a rainbow, representing financial success. We see the face of our successful man and we also see the castle his prosperity has built. Above all of this is a peacock with his tail fanned in spectacular fashion.

In some cultures, the peacock is a symbol of good luck, where in others it is the reverse. This is a very ambivalent card. In it we see our own personal success but ultimately, money doesn't bring happiness in its own right. If you were happy and stable originally, then money will only serve to make life easier and happier. If you were lonely at the start of your journey, money can't buy you the affirmation you need.

Take two successful business owners who both have many friends. At first glance they would appear similar, but as you get to know them, you begin to understand a fundamental difference. The first is relatively secure in his own sense of identity and worth. He has many friends and continues to enlarge his social circle. He has recently met the man of his dreams and they are soon to become civil partners. He has frequent house parties for his friends which are unique, happy affairs. Everyone goes home feeling enriched and refreshed. He is a truly generous host and an overall remarkable man.

The second man also has regular parties for large numbers of friends but the guest list is constantly shifting. Many of the men he mixes with seem to take advantage of his good nature and his finances. He eventually enters a civil partnership, but a couple of his long-standing friends express reservations about his partner's motives for marrying him. They suspect he has been married for his money.

Two wealthy men, both partnered and both with extensive social circles. The latter however is deeply insecure about his own self-worth, spending his life being financially generous for the wrong reasons.

You can't buy friendship or respect. What he really bought were superficial friends who took advantage of his generosity. These usually disappear when the wallet runs dry.

This is the conundrum of the nine of pentacles. Material gain is good, but it isn't an end in itself. How are you using your wealth? Recognize that for all the time you've invested in your material welfare, an equal amount of time must be spent nurturing your emotional wellbeing and that of those close to you. Castles can be a very lonely place if there's only one man living in each of them.

MATERIAL GAIN

$\mathcal{T}$en pentacles form the spheres on the Kabbalistic tree of life. From the bottom sphere where heavenly energy manifests in earthly form, the light of the sun shines brightly. This warmth and glow hovers above the earth, filling it with light and life. In the clouds, we see the faces of four men. They may be partners, they may be friends. Whatever they are they are bound together in love and acceptance.

This card is about true wealth. Unlike the gain shown in the Nine of Pentacles, this is fulfilled prosperity. It is our gain, sent out to our friends, loved ones, and the wider world and then received back tenfold.

In Kabbalah, the tree of life is a diagram showing how the divine lightning strike traces its path from heaven to earth. At each fork or junction of that lightning strike, a divine emanation or Sephirah manifests in spherical form. To represent these spheres as pentacles is to use the tree as a symbol for material wholeness, unity, and fulfillment. Material wealth, be it in financial riches, abundance of food, bodily health or sexual/sensual gratification is a gift not to be taken

for granted. Our riches are a divine blessing, not an automatic right.

Wealth always functions at its best when shared. We enjoy our riches, but for me, there's a double enjoyment in seeing others enjoy them, too. When we share selflessly, we enjoy the full benefits of our gains.

Traditional cards often show a wealthy family in a castle courtyard. For many gay men, the families we build for ourselves from our gay friends increasingly become the most important family units as we grow older. I am lucky to have an accepting family, but some of my friends have not been so lucky. In the most extreme case, one friend was so badly assaulted by his father when he came out that he suffered a broken arm. Such gay men would be alone except for the unspoken family adoption that often goes on between friends. Gay men become mothers, fathers, brothers, and sisters to each other in such circumstances. Luckily, some of the happiest Christmas tables I've ever seen have been surrounded by such men who have formed their own surrogate families. They understand true wealth. They

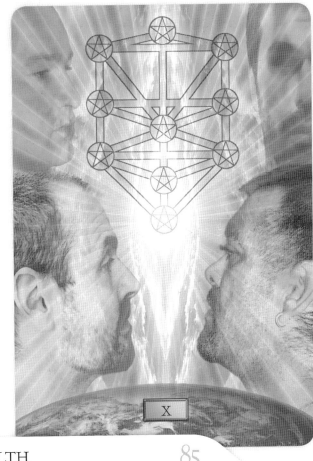

understand a healthy and laden table shared with those who love you unconditionally.

Where can you make a difference? How can you make your wealth come alive by sharing it? If this card appears, look at your family, friends, and support networks. Ask if you're giving out as much as you're receiving. Wealth is about enjoying the full fruits of divine blessing, but it's equally about using the gifts of the gods to spread a little happiness. Your own happiness will be increased as a result.

X

WEALTH

Swords represent the element of Air and here we see both the root of the element and all the powerful new beginnings it can bring in our lives.

Air is the element of the mind so the sword represents mental clarity and the ability to cut through to the truth. It is also a symbol of conflict and battle so the suit of Swords represents our personal battles and our quest for truth, integrity, and recognition.

We experience the first stroke of the sword when we choose to come out. As gay men in the closet, we have previously lived under a web of untruth, deception, fear of rejection, and prejudice. In choosing to deliberately lay bare the truth of our nature to family, friends, and society, the sword simultaneously frees us from the web and launches us into battle. It's liberating to be free of all the lies, but most of us will discover that coming out can only ever be the beginning of a whole new fight.

The Sword is a powerful symbol of our coming out experiences, but its significance as an archetype in our lives is so much wider. It's a symbol of liberation. In the card image, we can see the murky, confused dreamscape of the human mind being shattered by a sword. Look closely and you'll also see butterflies being set free as the sword cuts through the confusion. Butterflies are a symbol of air, but more importantly, the emerging butterfly is a symbol of transformation and freedom. In the realm of the mind, swords are all about the transformative trials we face in our lives. Conflict is a painful thing and very often we, as gay men, can be drawn in to prejudicial conflict we haven't asked for. There can also be conflict within our interpersonal relationships, but we mustn't forget to realize in all the pain and unpleasantness that we are in the midst of growth.

If the Ace of Swords appears in your reading, don't shy away from conflict, despite the pain it brings. These are the trials of life and you will grow in wisdom if you approach them with humility and an open mind. This is not always about winning, but it is about fighting for what's right and true. It's not always about fighting for yourself, either. We mature as we put other people first and fight to protect their rights and needs as well as our own. Your own coming out experience may be

ACE OF SWORDS

something long in the past, it may be recent, or you may even yet have to take that step. Don't fear it if that's the case, for you'll find life to be one long coming out process. It certainly won't be the last battle for truth, recognition, or justice that you'll engage in.

Under a waxing moon signifying rising tension, a man shuts his eyes tightly whilst crossing his arms firmly across his chest. It's as if he's trying to shield his heart from pain and his eyes from seeing the truth. A white dove of peace flies away and two swords are planted blade down before him. On one level, this card symbolizes peace, but the kind of peace represented by the Two of Swords is an uneasy state of being which requires great effort to maintain. The *Golden Dawn* named this card "Peace Restored," a title that further illustrates the effort put into calming a stormy situation.

This is the kind of denial that comes with the truth being withheld from those who need to hear it. To the outward world, an individual's circumstances and everyday life can appear to be happy, but such a man lives a constant and stressful balancing act to prevent himself or those around him from facing reality.

When this card appears in a reading, it invariably denotes denial, either in your own life or in the life of someone near to you. In gay culture, nothing exemplifies this more than being in the closet. Growing up in the North of England, in the 1970s and 1980s, involved the experience of acute cultural homophobia. I hid my true nature, living a double life that also involved misplaced religious beliefs and commitments. Several of my gay friends over the years hid within marriages. They married through peer or family pressure, and in several cases, genuinely believed that marriage would "fix" things.

Our denial and defense mechanisms actually cost us more dearly and took more effort to maintain than facing the truth would have done. Of course, this isn't always the case. Some men would jeopardize their careers and livelihoods if they came out of the closet. Others are forced to lie to protect their very lives. If you live in a country where homosexual acts are still illegal or where fundamentalist spiritual beliefs hold sway over civil society, then honesty is not an option.

Peace restored can also point to the quest for reconciliation. When somebody has hurt you, it can take an incredible act of will to forgive, yet for the sake of our own inner health, this can often be an essential step to take. The dove is a symbol of truth, but it is also a symbol of peace and forgiveness. The man in the card has loosed the dove, but it will be a slow process to uncover his wounded heart again. A wise man only uncovers a previously wounded heart with prudence.

When this card appears for you, examine yourself and those areas of secrecy in your life. What is the true cost of honesty? It may be the case that your shielding yourself and others from the truth no longer serves a healthy purpose. If deception comes at a high cost for you and your loved ones, then it's probably the time to face the truth.

TWO OF SWORDS

PEACE RESTORED

This is a traumatic image. Storms rage, lightning flashes, and explosions occur. All of this seems to emanate from within the man on the card. He's screaming with anguish. We can see a fractured heart with a tearful eye at its center and three upright swords conducting the energy of his pain.

Anyone who has experienced bereavement or the loss of a loved one will instinctively empathize with the pain in this card. Anyone who has suffered the collapse of a partnership or deep romantic relationship will know it, too. This is the card of heartbreak and sorrow. It feels like life is at war with you and your heart has been pierced by a thousand swords.

Human beings have an amazing way of "internalizing" those we love. When we are separated by physical distance, we don't normally suffer physical or emotional distress. Our sense of well-being is maintained by the imprint of our loved ones on our heart and the recollections of their faces in our head. With a lover, we can close our eyes and imagine their arms around us and all the attendant sensations of loving intimacy. Under such circumstances, we barely register the vast geographical distances between ourselves and those we love, despite our rational understanding of what it means to be hundreds, or sometimes even a thousand, miles away. We may miss them terribly, but somehow they remain close.

Grief and sorrow strip us of those securities. Divorce, relationship collapse, or bereavement leaves the heart isolated. We don't have the security of knowing that whatever the distance, that person is still there for us. We are on our own and it's a cold place to be. Sorrow like this can shatter our very being and often it takes months or years, along with the care and support of those around us, to piece our lives back together. Grief is a journey with an end however. The important thing is to flow with the process. Cry when you need to cry, be angry when you need to be angry, and most difficult of all, let go when the time comes to move on. The best way to honor the memory of the dead is to carry on living a fulfilled life. The best way to make sense of a failed relationship is to learn from it and to forge a new life for yourself. Like a storm or a blizzard, grief must always pass and give way to new light and life.

SORROW

This card is very much about retreating from the real world to clear your head, recharge your batteries, and to decide where you go from here.

With the last card, we talked about grief and trauma. If you've lost your partner or if you've lost your job, it's sometimes essential to have time out so you can still your mind and regain a rational slant on the world. The card image itself is very much one of escapism. The man sleeps, hidden within the clouds. The sun shines through an almost heavenly stained-glass window whilst four swords hang at rest above him.

In days gone by, churches were traditionally a place of "sanctuary." If you took refuge under the wings of the church, neither your enemies or the powers of the land could cross the threshold to touch you. There are valid times in life where we need to hide following major upsets or change. Sometimes, a holiday or a weekend away will be enough. At other times, it only takes to turn off the phone or not answer the door. There are occasions, however, when the need for sanctuary requires more long-term measures. It may be that this card indicates the need for a fresh start in a new town or city. You may be running away for a month, a year, or even for ten years. You may never return. Whatever the case, a move like this is sometimes necessary to find your peace of mind.

When this card appears, it's an indicator to take some down time or time away. If life has become a struggle, it's probably time to re-group and take stock. Be prepared for change. Very often, periods of retreat like this can lead to transformations in your life as you find yourself re-energized and re-empowered. We begin to see things from new and different angles once we're out of the everyday cross fire. Having found our solutions, we're ready to put them into effect.

REST FROM STRIFE

The image on this card shows the outcome of a particularly nasty war of words. There's a very obvious victor whose arrogance is expressed by the obscenity of his hand gesture. There's also an obvious victim whose shattered confidence can be seen in his slumped shoulders and head hung low. The card represents the concept of defeat, but it's also about the dynamics of conflict and our attitudes towards it.

Considering the large amount of discrimination, hatred, and persecution often leveled at our community of gay men from the outside, it still amazes me how good we are at hitting the self-destruct button from within. How can we criticize the straight community for victimizing gay men when we have been busy victimizing each other? Camp bitchiness, ageism, and body fascism have frequently taken their cancerous toll on many a man when directed straight at him from the mouths of other gay men. It's horrifying to see the emerging confidence of a man exploring his gay identity cut down in a flash because in someone's mind he's supposedly too old, too fat, too thin, too ugly, too square, too boring, too unfashionable… The list goes on.

My journey into my life as a happy and fulfilled gay man has been a rewarding one. I'm lucky to have met and befriended some of the most amazing, talented, and loving men you could ever wish to have in your life. Early on, though, I discovered a side of the gay lifestyle that I struggled to deal with. This was precisely the shallow and critical mindset that some gay men allow themselves to slip into. I couldn't compete in the arena of the gym bunny or the disco bunny, and I quickly realized that I had no desire to either. The quest for eternal youth and the body of Adonis showed itself to be a cruelly competitive one where the outer shell meant everything and what was on the inside counted for nothing.

In the past, I've been just as guilty of ageist attitudes and other forms of prejudice towards men who didn't quite fit my bill. Thankfully, life's hard knocks made me re-examine my own bad attitudes, but like everyone, I probably need a lot more challenging. That's what the appearance of this card means for all of us in a reading. Who are you in this card? Are you the arrogant man with his middle finger in the air?

Just who are you undermining in your life? Can you really justify your prejudice and behavior? Alternately, maybe you're the vanquished guy on his knees. Do you really need to be there? Take a look at the person who's done this to you. Think about their attitudes and words. Are they really as valid as you think? Do you really need to take so many negatives on board?

When this card appears, look to cultivate some mutual understanding and respect with the men you struggle with the most. A little tolerance and compassion goes a long way, and after all, we're in this together.

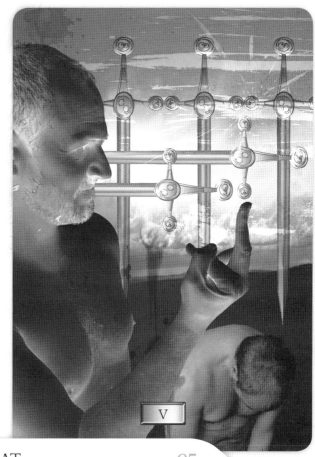

FIVE OF SWORDS

V

DEFEAT

SIX OF

Sometimes this card is called "Earned Success." The Crowley *Thoth Tarot* calls it "Science," whilst the *Rider Waite Tarot* shows the image of a boat, ferrying its two passengers across stormy waters towards a calm and tranquil island.

However many levels this card functions on, its message is beautiful and affirming. At its heart, it's about positive advancement. Through hard strife, you've earned the joy of moving on to a better place. In our card, a ship sails into the rising sun as a new morning dawns. Six swords emerge from the water, showing a path to the sunrise and we see a man who's inner spirit manifests as a swan – calm, regal, and graceful – as it sails across the waters.

Six marks a sense of completion, and in this card, it's the sense of a difficult journey coming to a close. You've reached peaceful waters after many struggles and battles. In practical terms, maybe you and your partner have recently endured a difficult spell in your relationship. After many challenges, much soul searching and surrendering your wills to each other, you've finally reached an equilibrium.

This is a new place, marked by maturity gained through hard experience. From here you can go from strength to strength.

In my own experience, this card has often signified that peaceful place reached when conflicts in friendships and relationships have been resolved. This does not necessarily happen quickly; sometimes it can take years, but there is a true feeling of release when old differences are finally settled and forgiveness is exchanged.

When this card appears in your reading, expect to move forward to a better place than the one you're in now. It's as if the universe recognizes the strife you've endured and it's gently nudging your circumstances forward, clearing away any stagnation and allowing you to sail ahead. It's a card of new beginnings and better times to come. Where difficult relationships are concerned, expect to see a breakthrough. The waters have now calmed sufficiently to allow your ship to set sail and it's time for this relationship to move forward to a new phase with you.

EARNED SUCCESS

Through the mist, smoke, and haze of a battlefield, a man creeps along the ground trying to evade detection. Five swords are silhouetted hanging in the air, two stand upright in the ground. Above him we can see the apparition of a fox, symbolizing stealth and caution. High above flies an eagle, whose far sight represents the risk of detection for the fugitive. Look even closer and you'll see the eyes of his enemies, constantly on the lookout.

Referred to in the *Golden Dawn Tarot* as the card of "Unstable Effort," the seven of swords symbolizes our efforts to remain afloat within an unstable environment. It also symbolizes the need for stealth and shows that it isn't always appropriate to tell the whole truth. There are times in your life where you will have to pick a precarious and diplomatic path through difficult circumstances or relationships.

Coming out to friends and family can be a liberating experience, but if the time isn't right, it can be an equally traumatic one. In some family circumstances, coming out may never be possible. One of my friends whose parents are now in their eighties remains firmly in the closet to them, despite being out to siblings, nephews, and nieces. The potential disruption at such a late stage in their lives far outweighs any possible benefits. Similarly, in some previous workplaces, I've been open about my sexuality because it hasn't been an issue. In others, I've remained secretive because I've known that the knowledge of my being a gay man would jeopardize my professional position.

Such secrecy shouldn't have to be a feature of the family or work place, but the reality is we still live in an age where liberal attitudes towards sexuality are partial and selective, depending on where you are.

In friendships and relationships, truth and transparency are usually the right option, but there are still occasions when white lies can be in your loved ones' best interests. It's immensely difficult to draw the line to say where lying becomes acceptable, but sometimes the full truth can cause unnecessary hurt to the ones you love. Tread carefully, but also ask yourself who your deceptions are serving. Are you protecting your loved one or simply protecting yourself? Only you can tell.

VII

UNSTABLE EFFORT

This card is dark and congested to the point of claustrophobia. A blindfolded man is hemmed in by eight swords, jagged edges, and thick tangled branches. He's swathed in darkness, and even if he wasn't blindfolded, he wouldn't be able to see the woods for the trees.

Whenever this card appears, it's indicating factors in your life that constrict you from functioning to your maximum. They blind you to the obvious and prevent you from asserting yourself in a healthy way. You can't fight for your corner because there simply isn't enough space to move forward.

If we're told lies for long enough, we often begin to believe them. Many gay men have grown into adulthood with the constant message of being somehow less than a real man. Of course, this is a lie, but more often than not, experiencing the fullness of your male identity requires belief in yourself and all the added confidence that can bring. What we see in this card is the cowardly use of the sword. Rather than fight directly, people are seeking to undermine your confidence in yourself. They don't have to limit or constrict your power; it's so much easier than that. They only have to condition you to limit yourself. This says more of the perpetrator's weakness than of your own, but as men, we are confronted with the stark choice of choosing to listen or choosing to re-claim our personal empowerment.

On another level, it's sometimes hard to fight through a difficult situation because you're too close to it all to be objective. When you can't take a step forward, it's sometimes advisable to take a step back so you can get a clearer picture of what's really going on. Relationships particularly can become the jagged and tangled mess we can see in the card. How often have you found yourself in love but hurting each other all the same? If you're in this confined and tangled space and you can't step forwards or backwards, just calm yourselves and stand still. Take stock, learn to name your obstacles and constrictions. Once you've done this, you may even find you have the power to remove them.

This is an unhealthy place to be but ultimately you can take heart. This isn't about not having the power or strength you need to live a happy and affirmed life. All the strength you need is within you. This is about external limitations and cages, and though it may require considerable courage, resources and soul searching, you can break free.

VIII

SHORTENED FORCE

This is one of the most difficult cards in the Tarot. With the Ace we saw the positive and victorious aspects of the suit. We have journeyed through heartache, trial and tribulation, but also through victory, rest and retreat, and earned success. What happens when the victory isn't ours? We've touched on this with the Five but with the Nine of Swords, we are finally faced with what appears to be a no-win situation.

The Nine of Swords represents the despair of being powerless and the cruelty of your enemies. The card itself shows a man in despair, trapped in a web of evil. Nine swords point inwards to the center of the web and a ravening beast bears his teeth behind him.

There are times in life when the only safe thing to do is to retreat and there's definitely no shame in that. If you find yourself in the place this card describes, it can take a great deal of bravery on your own part to admit defeat or to admit your complete lack of power. This is one of the greatest disciplines of true manhood; mastering the art of embracing personal weakness. When a man can forgive himself for being weak, he really has become strong in the best possible sense.

Domestic violence is a good example of the nature of this card. In a situation like this, a staged retreat is good for both yourself and for the ultimate good of your partner. Maybe your partner has drug or alcohol dependency issues. Loving support can go so far, but ultimately, your partner must face his demons on his own and for himself. If he is unwilling to do that, you will find yourself dragged down to the point where two lives will be destroyed. Such situations are difficult to call and you will find yourself making heart-rending decisions. If this is the case, draw on the wisdom of those you trust, and above all, on the advice of professionals who have your interests at heart as well as those of your partner.

Life can be wonderful, but there are times when life can be unbelievably cruel. In such situations we must often pay a high personal cost. There's no shame in self-preservation. If you have to admit defeat and stage a retreat in the face of cruelty, then you've taken the brave step of recognizing your limitations and learning to value your own wellbeing. In such a case, you've done the manly thing and being the loser carries no dishonor.

There is another important aspect of this card. It has to do with facing our own inner demons. Maybe there are moments in your past that fill you with horror or cause you to wake at night in a cold sweat. Some traumas run deep and if this is the case with you, then the message is to go gently. Some terrors can't be faced quickly and many can't be faced alone. This card is a call to acknowledge the dark fears that may color your life, but at the same time, this is a call to be both gentle and patient with yourself.

VIIII

DESPAIR AND CRUELTY

At the start of this suit, we were faced with the optimistic ace with its promises of victory and freedom. Here at the end of the sequence, we find the opposite state where there is only defeat and ruin. This is a hard reality to bear, but wherever there is endeavor or wherever we have a battle on our hands, defeat and ruin is always a possibility. This is possibly the saddest card in the Tarot because it really does depict that dreadful place in our lives where all else has failed. These are those devastating times in life where the world lies in ruin around you and there's nothing you can do to put it back together again. Retreat isn't even an option here. We've simply lost and this is the end of the line.

In the card we see a man pierced through the heart by a sword. He sinks beneath the waves as he dies and his blood stains the waters red. This card isn't all about doom, however. Only a single sword has caused such a mortal wound in our lives. The remaining nine swords rise renewed with the sun on the horizon. A painful ending may have occurred in our lives, but these nine swords show that we will live to fight another day victorious.

When you draw this card, remember the painful fact that we can't win them all. Each year brings its joys, but it will also bring a large share of inevitable sorrows. Both are an essential part of our lives. When ruin occurs, embrace the pain. It's almost impossible to see at the time, but our lives are like a tree being pruned. Branches are lost but in the grand scheme of things, this pruning is essential for new growth to flourish. Your personal catastrophe can be a turning point, but ultimately, only you can make the decision to make it so.

X

RUIN

A red hot wand flies through the air and shatters a window. Through the glass we see a maelstrom of fire, its flames forming the facial features of a man. Like some tribal magician, he wears a headdress shaped like a tiger. This reflects his inner core, as the tiger is a symbol of fire. This figure is the origin of fire and the Wand is his talismanic symbol. The Ace shows us all the aspects of ourselves ruled by fire. First and foremost, fire within the body and heart of a man is the "libido" energy. This isn't just to do with our sex drive; libido is our creative, pro-creative, and re-creative energies in their widest sense. Where sexual energy is concerned, the wand is an overt phallic symbol. The Ace as a symbol of beginnings deals with our sexual awakening; something we all experience in unique and diverse ways. Some men say they always knew they were gay, others speak of an age when they first knew. Not only does the Ace symbolize our first awareness of our sexuality, it also symbolizes our first experiences.

For some men drawing this card, may be the awakening is only just beginning. The discovery of hidden feelings and passions isn't always reserved for the innocence of youth. For an experienced man, it can also denote the appearance in your life of a man who will fan the flames of your inner desires and open your sexual awareness in a whole new way. In entering a new relationship, you discover the power of your libido to be deeper and wider than you thought.

On a wider level, the Ace of Wands can also represent birth. It can be a literal symbol of the birth of a child; the culmination of man's procreative drives. On a more practical level, it can too symbolize the adoption of a child and the beginning of that child's life with its new parents. As gay men wanting children, this is the most practical route that most of us can take. We may not be physically giving birth, but we are still creatively giving birth to a new family unit.

On a purely creative level, the Ace of Wands embodies the source of our creative powers. Whether we are artists, sculptors, writers, musicians, skilled craftsmen, builders, or workmen trained in any other occupation, the creative energy of the Ace allows us to give birth to the ideas, inspirations, and concepts in our minds and hearts.

At its highest level, fire is the element of the spirit and the Ace denotes that hidden fire within all of us. To experience sacred fire is to enter the unseen reality of the gods, the goddesses, the angels, the ancestors, and the spirits of the earth. Whatever your faith or your beliefs, the Ace shows the awakening of your hidden, transcendent self and your calling to a higher purpose.

ACE OF WANDS

ACE OF WANDS

A man holds a world in his hands and sparks fly from two wands, blazing like torches. Within the flames, you can see emblems of a rose and a lily. In the realm of fire, two is the number of potential. Crowley calls it the card of "Dominion." With the world in your hands, this card tells you that anything is possible.

Male potential is both exciting and awesome. We are each an awesome and wondrous force of nature, but how many of us have explored even a fraction of this? Fire is the most masculine of elements, yet many gay men have grown up with the misconception that to be gay is somehow to be less than male. We're often made to believe that to be gay is to be effeminate and to be effeminate is to be weak. If effeminacy equates with being womanlike, surely this isn't a weakness. Women are remarkable beings with even more remarkable reserves of inner strength. Old-fashioned homophobia has no insight into the souls of true men. It is also eminently misogynistic as it connects being woman like with being inferior. It's time to banish such unhealthy voices and internalize a new and healthier script to our lives. Many gay men have an unusual affinity with women and understand them from a unique perspective. In a strange, sometimes mystical way, gay men and lesbians bridge the gulf between men and women. We are members of one physical sex yet we have some of the traits and drives of the other. This is no gender diminishing weakness. It is pure strength.

Whatever shape and size you are, whether you feel confident or not, begin to accept that you are uniquely and powerfully male. How do you feel inside? How does your body feel physically? Whatever you feel, these are the sensations connected to being male. Touch your face, stroke your hair, savor the moment. Above all, think of the strongest and most masculine man you know, then affirm this truth: You're as male as he is. You're his equal and you're just as precious, not because you're the same as him, not because you're better than someone else, but simply because you're unique. In the vast time span that constitutes the history of the Universe, there will only ever be one man like you. That kind of uniqueness is too precious to demean.

The Two of Wands symbolizes the potential of your masculinity and the power of your inner fire. You have the power to create and shape in a miraculous way. Your sex drive allows you to channel spiritual and sensual fire as a gift to other men in the most mystical and miraculous way. You can be a channel for love, passion, creativity, joy, and fervor. None of us can achieve everything, but your potential as a man is far greater and more wondrous than you've ever realized. Lift a flaming torch in each hand and begin to be the amazing man you were created to be.

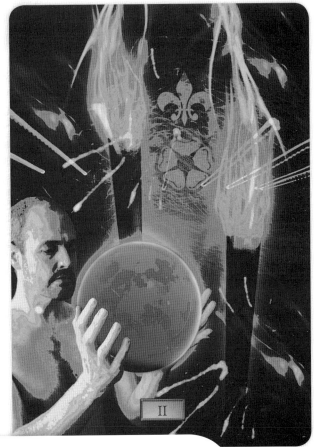

TWO OF WANDS

Once you've realized your potential, it's time to establish your strength and begin to realize your dreams. This card is about beginning to manifest your talents, moving confidently in your masculinity, and setting the wheels in motion to achieve your goals.

The sky and water alike are charged with fire energy in this card. Three towering wands stand as a monument to this man's ambitions. His goals are still far off on the horizon and he must walk through waters of uncertainty to reach them, yet his journey is well under way. Human potential has been manifested and set in motion.

Writing this book was a manifestation of the Three of Wands. When this project was first conceived in 2005, I was to illustrate the cards, but the well-known Tarot writer and deck creator Lee Bursten was to write the accompanying book. Several publishers turned us down along the way, and latterly, Lee had to pull out of the project due to other commitments.

It seemed strange to me, but Lee realized that in reality this wasn't a project for him.

"Only you can write this book," were his words to me. I felt daunted by the whole thing and unsure I could see it through. The deck itself has seen two major revisions since that time. The images have become enriched, the concept has become more complex in some ways, more straightforward in others. Over a six-year period, *The Son Tarot* evolved and matured to what it is now. For several months after my contract was signed, I hesitated to put pen to paper. I eventually began writing whilst on holiday. The first few hundred words were a hesitant affair, but by the end of my week away, I had ten thousand words drafted. As you get further into a journey like this, confidence increases.

This card is very much about pushing the boat out and exploring beyond your comfort zone. You may also be challenged to explore the fiery realm of your sexual energies. A friend of mine, having emerged from a stagnant, seventeen-year relationship found the courage to book himself on a weekend workshop teaching Tantric skills for gay men. His heart knew what the Two of Wands had already told him in a Tarot reading some weeks earlier. He had deep potentials he'd never explored. This workshop was his voyage towards realizing those potentials and discovering untouched parts of himself. Two things hallmarked the weekend for him. Firstly, an earth-shattering orgasm taught him his body could give him experiences he never dreamed could exist. Secondly, with the correct channeling of his sexual energy came floods of tears. These were tears of grief, tears of wonder, and tears of joy all mixed together. He had finally begun a long overdue journey towards his goals of sexual, emotional, and spiritual integration.

When this card appears, be brave, take hold of the potential you've seen engendered by the Two of Wands, and set it in motion towards clear goals. Like a rolling stone gathering momentum, so potential gathers speed and confidence. You'll find the journey is just as important a process as achieving your goals.

III

THREE OF WANDS

Though four is a number of stability, fire is the most dynamic of the elements. In this realm, stability manifests through joy and celebration.

Traditionally, this card has often symbolized a wedding. In the *Rider Waite Tarot,* the illustration even shows a four-pillared wedding canopy, garlanded with fruit and flowers. Our card is not much different. It depicts the joy and celebration behind a gay marriage or civil partnership.

Four glowing wands form the pillars of the wedding canopy but rather than fruit and flowers, this canopy is garlanded with rainbows – our community's symbol of liberty and freedom. The air around the canopy is incandescent with fire and fireworks. The loving couple embrace joyfully and affectionately. Finally, glowing with golden light, we can see two intertwined wedding rings in the center of the rainbows.

The official and legally recognized marriage of two men is both cause for celebration and a completion on several levels. Firstly, our community has fought for this right in many countries for many years. Although discrimination still exists in places and much still

needs to be fought for, we are lucky in many European countries and in parts of America. We can now enjoy the legal recognition and privileges afforded to heterosexual couples. We can outwardly validate our love and commitment within society at last.

On a personal level, to marry your lover and soul mate is to say, "I love you for life" in a way we've not previously been able to do. For some couples, this may not be important. Among my own friends, one couple, together for over twenty years, can see no need to make an outward declaration of their love. For them, there is nothing to prove, although they recognize the benefits and legal stability civil partnership could give them. On the other hand, other couples can finally make what they see as a precious and binding commitment to each other, in the eyes of their friends, family, and the wider society.

Marriage is a truly beautiful thing when it's between two people meant for each other. It's definitely the cause for celebration, but this kind of completion is not an end in itself. It's only the beginning of a new and more important phase. When the celebrations die down and the honeymoon is over, a loving couple must embark on their new life together.

When the Four of Wands appears, your efforts have been rewarded and your potential has seen its initial realization. This could be within a relationship or maybe within a work or creative project. Maybe it's the culmination of a wish. It could be a first date with the guy you've been keen on for months. Maybe it's the first time you've slept together and you've formed an unspoken bond. Such powerful culminations can only open doors to new and greater chapters. Enjoy your moment of celebration but remember the hard work begins here and greater things lie ahead.

IIII

COMPLETION

This card introduces us to the personal struggles that form an essential part of our growth and development.

Five wands form a tangled clash of energies as they merge with the surrounding flames and sparks. Within this maelstrom, we can see a man fighting with his alter ego. Blue fire and orange fire collide as two strong and equally stubborn wills are pitted against each other.

My own development as a gay man seems to have been a constant struggle between my ideals and my inextinguishable emotional immaturity. When I look back, my coming out process was dogged by misguided and foolish religious ideals. My thirties were characterized by a string of unsuitable partners and broken relationships. My stubbornness and inflexibility has often been my downfall.

There is a fundamental difference between who I am now and the person I was ten years ago. I don't justify my faults, but I can now look at myself in all my inadequacy and say, "Welcome to the human race."

Have I learned from my mistakes? Maybe not all of them, but I've learned from some of them. Am I any less foolish than I was ten years ago? The answer is maybe. Whatever the case, I'm learning to overcome different kinds of foolishness than I was back then.

We need to struggle with ourselves to grow. We're only evolving as long as our struggles and mistakes hold a harsh mirror in front of us. Most men wish they hadn't made so many mistakes or hurt so many people as they learned to mature. In the absence of learning the easy way, however, we seem to learn best the hard way.

When you look back at your mistakes, see them in a constructive light. As in sport, some fights promote fitness. Seemingly silly mistakes in the past can be the greatest learning experiences. If you changed as a result of a mistake, then it has done its job. Growth and evolution are a painful business but the birth process and pain go hand in hand. Don't live to regret, just live to learn.

FIVE OF WANDS

In this image, we see symbols of victory in several areas and walks of life where gay men have won recognition in the face of adversity. We see symbols of the military, sport, and the same interlocking wedding rings we saw on the Four of Wands, representing gay marriage. At the center of it all we see the outline of a rugby player emblazoned with the rainbow flag and crowned with a laurel wreath. In the culture of the British Isles, rugby has traditionally been regarded as one of our toughest, most masculine national sports.

In December 2009, Gareth "Alfie" Thomas, an ex-captain of the Welsh national rugby team, came out as a gay man to the British press. He was one of the first top-level sports personalities to do so. Since then, Steven Davies of England's national cricket team has done the same. Men like these are living proof of what gay men can accomplish in the world of professional sport. There is still much to achieve, but the sporting world is finding itself under increasing pressure to tackle discriminatory attitudes towards us.

Back in 2002, I was privileged to meet one of the men who had been brave enough to take the British Ministry of Defense to court to challenge his dismissal on the grounds of sexual orientation. Because of his bravery in making a stand, gay men and women can now serve openly within our armed forces without fear of discrimination.

These men are my personal heroes. They banish stereotypes and their courage in their convictions clears the way for us to excel and achieve where previously we would not have been welcome. Their example has given me the long-overdue realization that I am capable of accomplishing far more than I ever would have believed. There is no denying that achievement and courage go hand in hand.

This card represents all the victories gay men have achieved and all the victories they are capable of achieving. It's a testament to the fact that we are vessels of masculine drive and energy, equal in stature to our heterosexual counterparts. If you find that hard to believe, it's only because you've yet to uncover it within yourself. Your sexual orientation may not be that of the majority, but you are no less of a hero because of it.

VICTORY

With the Five of Wands, we saw constructive struggle and strife; the kind of trials we face as an essential part of our growth. With the Seven we see outright opposition that requires all our energies and bravery to stand up to. This is the card of trials. It is the card of valor.

In the card, we see our man wielding a white-hot wand defending himself against the six others being used to attack him. When this card appears, the stakes are high and you are faced with make-or-break opposition. It also symbolizes the dangerous and sometimes life-threatening opposition faced by gay men past and present around the world. In many Western European and American territories, we take our freedoms and liberties as gay men for granted. This isn't the case in other parts of the world. Steven Monjeza and Tiwonge Chimbalanga were imprisoned in Malawi in 2010 for holding a gay marriage ceremony. Think of Uganda – a society which, as I write, is trying to forward a parliamentary bill recommending the death sentence for certain "persistent" homosexual offenses.

As a teenager, I found myself in radicalized Evangelical spheres where I misguidedly learned my sexuality was something to be exorcised or healed. I largely broke free from such influences by my early thirties, but it took until I was almost forty for the residual guilt and fear attached to my church experiences to be fully dealt with.

Such opposition seeks to undermine our validity as human beings to the very core. It goes beyond genuine religion and spirituality. It's simply grounded in taboo, ignorance, and fear. Opposition like this requires inner strength to overcome along with the patient help and support from friends. I count myself lucky as my struggle was only on a personal and religious community level. By contrast, two of my Middle Eastern friends found themselves fleeing their respective countries, fearing for their lives when their sexuality was disclosed.

This card highlights the frightening side of our struggles, but it's also a testament to some of the heroes within our community. One only has to think of the work of organizations like Stonewall, fighting for gay rights and equality. Regardless of what many people think of the tactics of English campaigner Peter Tatchell in his younger days, most people would admit that he's grown to become a gay rights and human rights campaigner of extraordinary determination and integrity. Let's celebrate these heroes in our community and look to them as role models when we're faced with our own serious trials, whatever they may be.

SEVEN OF WANDS

VII

The message of this card is simple. This is unimpeded fire.

These are the times in your life when progress seems to surge forward with no obstacles in its path. Something you've dreamed of for years finally takes shape and your life moves forward in a new way. In the realm of love, whatever it is that keeps you and your partner separate has now disappeared and you can begin your new life together. For someone who is single, this can be the moment when that special person enters your life without warning. The tempo quickens, and suddenly, you're on a rollercoaster of change and discovery

On a creative level, writers and artists will deeply empathize with this card as it symbolizes the moment a creative block is removed. You spend weeks, even months, unable to give form to your creative inspiration, then suddenly, it pours out over page or canvas. Sexually, this refers to those moments of perfect alignment where the sexual energies of two people seem to entwine totally, and for that surreal moment, you almost feel you could fly. The energy here is an adrenalin rush of explosive power and you feel yourself swept along. You're almost out of control but for the moment, it's unimportant.

When you draw this card, expect a rush of activity as doors are unlocked, hand brakes removed, and obstacles flattened. Don't try to control what's going on, just allow yourself to be swept up. Wherever you're carried is where you are destined to be. Where a broken heart is concerned, it may be time for the floodgates to open within you. You'll find yourself experiencing pain and grief that you've long kept at bay. Despite the pain, let it flow, for now is the time for healing. When the tidal wave of grief subsides, you'll find yourself in a peaceful place.

EIGHT OF WANDS

VIII

SWIFTNESS

A wounded man clings firmly to one of nine wands as a fire storm rages around him. This is his only stability within a turbulent environment, but he is determined to persevere, even though he needs to draw on his deepest reserves of endurance to do so.

The *Golden Dawn's* title of "Great Strength" doesn't refer to the inner fire and life force that we encountered in the Major Arcana. It talks about something more personal. This is the human quality of endurance in the face of adversity. It's the courage that somehow carries us through even the darkest of places.

The man in the card could almost be under siege. He's certainly isolated and only by using his deepest reserves to cling to the known areas of stability in his life can he hope to survive. Maybe you've been in an abusive relationship that has systematically eroded your confidence and self-worth. Maybe it's time to stage a retreat. Whatever the case, you're bruised but not broken and the wands represent those people or places that can give you true anchorage in the storm. The wands also symbolize the setting of healthy boundaries. By planting them firmly in the ground before you, you are giving a clear message to "come this far, but no further." Post conflict or coming out of an abusive relationship, this kind of boundary setting is an essential part of re-building your life. Not only are you putting in place a framework for your own protection, you are also re-claiming the right to set your own rules. You are re-gaining your confidence and the ability to say no. Furthermore, you are setting up the healthy barriers that will protect your emotional and physical welfare in the future.

If you've been a victim of homophobic bullying or discrimination, this card is about learning to take back control of your destiny. It's fine to be wounded. This isn't weakness. The wounded are often the strong with scars. When you realize this, you also begin to discover your own healthy stubbornness. You can plant your feet firmly on the ground and refuse to move should you wish to. Bullies thrive on the fear of others because they are weak. Show your strength and you'll be amazed at how quickly they crumble.

When opposition is just too much and you find yourself out of your depth, there's no shame in retreat.

At times like this, we plant the wands as a defensive barrier to hide behind. Sometimes, you just have to admit defeat and walk away. At times like these, this is the strongest thing to do. Strength is also about knowing your own limitations. Sometimes we fight; sometimes we take flight so that we can fight another day.

When this card appears, look to your inner strength and endurance, but beware of misusing it. Enduring abuse when you need to retreat or leave permanently is a dangerous thing to do. Likewise, protecting someone you love from the consequences of their own behavior and taking the damage on yourself leaves a question mark over your motives. Loving someone does not mean enabling them to behave wrongly. Sometimes love must be tough love. How far will you go?

NINE OF WANDS

GREAT STRENGTH

A man is weighed down as he carries the weight of the whole world on his shoulders. Ten wands bear down on the world and crush him even further. Maybe you need to learn to carry your life challenges in a more effective way.

Sometimes we feel we just can't function any more. The weight of the world gets too much to carry and we buckle beneath it. This oppression can often manifest through past hurts controlling the present. If you grew up in a homophobic environment or you inherited a burden of disapproval from your family, then maybe you're still living for other people's expectations and not your own. Before long, life can seem like a ball and chain and your true hopes and aspirations begin to wither through lack of nourishment. It's all too easy to lose our will to live a full and happy life when we internalize other people's disapproval. We cannot carry other people's emotional baggage forever. There comes a time when you must learn to live for yourself and for your own unique destiny. If some of those close to you disapprove, it's just too bad.

Look at your life with total honesty and ask yourself who really makes the decisions. We only get one life and we only have one chance of fulfilling our unique purpose. If you draw this card, it suggests a loss of fulfillment and happiness in your life because you're conforming to a pattern that doesn't fit you. You can't live life through someone else's blueprint. To do so places a world on your shoulders you were never designed to carry. Is it any wonder you struggle? Be true to yourself.

OPPRESSION

The face of a man is a window onto the world of water. The sun casts its rays through the clouds onto a boundless ocean and from the waters a single cup emerges. Framing the center of the man's face is the unbroken downward triangle; the Alchemical symbol for water.

Water is the element of the emotions, the soul, and the intuitive capacity. This is the element of instinct and the unconscious. We see the ocean on the card as a man's inner world for the suit of Cups deals with our feelings and our inner being. As the element of the heart it is also the element of love.

These are the same waters that we see in the Moon card, but here they are at peace, basking in the light of the Sun. The cup emerging from the ocean is the manifestation of our feelings in the real world. It is our offering of love to our beloved. Similarly, it can also be our offering of compassion and empathy to a friend in need.

In its most powerful manifestation, the Cup is a symbol of a new beginning and of a new emotional journey. It can indicate a psychic awakening or the forging of a particular empathic connection with another. Water is also the most basic element of life. It is essential for our survival, but it is also the growth medium in which new life can thrive. The Ace represents emotional potential not yet realized. It is our capacity to love held in readiness for when the Cup is offered for someone else to drink from it.

The Cup as a receptacle is a deeply feminine symbol, so here it speaks not only of our ability to give, but also of our ability to receive. This is the part of us that opens inwards to receive the love of others. It is also the open door through which the psyche of another can flow, his emotions blending with ours as a river blends with the sea.

When this card appears in your reading, switch off your mind and listen to your heart. The Ace of Cups is the root of "feminine" wisdom – the intuitive, instinctive ways of knowing that go beyond rational analysis. It is a call for you to open your heart, both to give and to receive. Many men find it difficult to come present to the reality of their emotions. They also find it difficult to share their emotions. This card is a call to present your heart to others as openly as the Cup rises from the ocean. It represents a new level of emotional honesty and transparency.

Trust your instincts. Dare to let your heart be open and vulnerable. Above all, your cup is waiting to be lifted to another man's lips. Dare to share and dare to let the waters of your soul flow freely with the souls of others.

ACE OF CUPS

ACE OF CUPS

Each OF OUR RELATIONSHIPS IS DIFFERENT, AND WE ARE DIFFERENT IN EACH OF THEM. THIS IS WHAT MAKES MONOGAMY SO PERVERSELY INTERESTING.

The above quote is something a very wise friend shared with me. This is the card of love and in particular, it's the card of one-on-one relationships. Two cups stand like great pillars, and between them, the sun rises over the ocean of the heart. Beneath the light of the sun, two young men dance a dance of love, mirroring each other's movements in admiration as they bask in the glow of sexual attraction. Emerging from the sun is a Caduceus crowned with a winged lion. You don't have to be young to experience the first flush of young love. It can sweep you away at any time of your life. It's when a man comes into your life and despite being merely human, he looks like your angel, your god, Adonis, and your hero all rolled into one. Furthermore, when he looks at you he sees exactly the same.

Two is the number of partnership and this card heralds the beginning of a new relationship or the re-affirmation of that glowing connection your partner engenders in you. Whether your relationship is old or new, you're aware of the fact that you're not alone in the most wonderful way. You've found the man you love and in him, you discover a strange sense of completion.

Whether it lasts or not, young love can be a profoundly healing experience. Like the winged lion, you feel as if you could achieve anything and fly anywhere. The Caduceus is the universal symbol of healing in the medical profession and here, it symbolizes the healing power of pure happiness. There are few things more healing or affirming than the warm strong arms of the man you love deeply wrapped round you in protection and adoration.

When this card appears, love is an issue or influence in your life. This is the time to open yourself and your soul to another and dare to love. If he's the right man for you, you'll know for sure. Love doesn't hesitate to recognize his soul mate and the touch of a hand or a gentle embrace can be the beginning of two men becoming one. Will it last? Who knows? Just take

the risk and enjoy the privilege of knowing him for a year, a day, or a lifetime. The old saying goes, "It is better to have loved and lost…"

Taste. Risk. Enjoy.

II

Here's a card with several layers of meaning. We can see three friends, three cups, celebratory fireworks and a six-pointed star, made up from the blue and orange triangles representing fire and water. In the Crowley *Thoth Tarot* and in the *Golden Dawn* tradition, this card is known as "Abundance," and on the simplest level, that's what it is – pure emotional abundance and joy to overflowing. When this card appears, we could be in the midst of a celebration or a party. Some Tarot readers even see it signifying a birth.

For us, as gay men, this card can work on several levels. Two is for couples whilst three represents that opening out of our focus from a partner or exclusive friendship to include third parties, so this card represents friendship in its dynamic form. This is where we learn to balance the needs of more than one party and spread our resources and loyalties between several. It also represents our ability as couples to share our energies outside of our monogamous partnerships. When you're single, you build up a social circle around yourself. As a couple you work together to draw in your existing friends so that they eventually accept and love your partner as they've always loved you. You also draw in new people together. "My friends" gradually become "Our friends" and that's a wonderful thing.

Three is also the number of "open" relationships, with all their inherent thrills, rewards, and dangers. Ask a group of gay men how they feel about monogamy versus the open relationship model and you'll get a raft of different answers. For many guys, their partner or husband is the one man in their life and there will never be another. On the other hand, some couples thrive on the extra excitement that opening their sex lives out to other men can bring. Some only "play together" whereas others will give each other the freedom to take other sexual partners separately. Some operate a "don't ask, don't tell" policy within this arrangement, whilst others have a policy of sexual freedom within the context of mutual transparency.

When the Three of Cups appears in your reading, celebrate your friendships, celebrate your lovers, or celebrate the freedoms of your open relationships. Whatever the case, these connections can only remain healthy with honesty and mutual respect. If there is any warning inherent in this card, it's to be aware of using the open relationship formula to avoid dealing with challenging intimacy issues between you and your partner. If you find yourself more attracted to your lover than your husband then it's time to ask questions.

THREE OF CUPS

III

$\mathcal{F}$our is the number of strength and stability. Crowley called this card "Luxury," denoting emotional abundance through stability, but I don't think this tells the whole story. Water, like the emotions, is a dynamic entity. It needs to flow or it will stagnate. Four as a number evokes foursquare containment and water is too dynamic an element to stay contained.

The *Golden Dawn* called this card "Blended Pleasure." Hermann Haindl probably summed it up best when he called his version of the card "Mixed Happiness." Stability is a good thing, but sometimes it leads to complacency and even stagnation. Have you gotten overly familiar with your partner? Has the stability and familiarity of your love led to the fires being extinguished? Maybe the castle you built together became so cozy that it's stopped being fun. This card shows you're content but bored.

The man in the card has three full cups and he's being offered a fourth as a divine gift. He just isn't interested anymore as he's got too much of a good thing. His desires are becoming frozen and he's trapped in the web of his own apathy. You don't have

to be in a complacent relationship to experience this, either.

Maybe you've been single for a long time and you've become disillusioned. You want a lover and a soul mate, but cynicism and past disappointments mean you've stopped looking. Maybe the right guy is there and being offered to you, but you're hurting too much from past experiences to want to take the risk on yet another potentially failed relationship.

Have you got yourself trapped in a cycle of casual sex and quick fixes? Casual sex can be fine in the right and healthy context, but the constant pursuit of instant gratification with a variety of different men can sometimes blind us to our deeper need for genuine intimacy.

Complacency is a difficult thing to deal with. Perhaps the highest wall to climb is the actual admission that something's wrong. After all, complacency can be a very safe place to be, even if it isn't that fulfilling. When this card appears in your reading, take a long hard look at what, if anything, is going stale in your life. Flowing water stays fresh, and in a similar way, the emotions must be allowed to flow selflessly from the heart to others so they can remain healthy. Whenever this kind of stagnancy starts to occur, we've inevitably stopped giving and receiving in the way that we should. Dare to let the boat be rocked again. Ask yourself some difficult questions, prepare to be challenged and above all, be open to change. You need to change and you need to grow to survive.

BLENDED PLEASURE   MIXED HAPPINESS

The *Golden Dawn Tarot* called this card "Loss in Pleasure." Aleister Crowley called it "Disappointment." Here's an example: Your boyfriend, who you worship like a golden idol, turns round and tells you he's been sleeping with your best friend. Furthermore, they are madly in love and you're being dumped. You're out in the cold and you've been betrayed on two counts. Can it really get any worse?

Look at our hero in the card. He's standing among the ruins of a once beautiful city and he's watching three cups that once contained his dreams floating away as their contents spill out. There are certain cards in the Tarot that spell out one of life's most profound truths: Shit happens.

Thankfully, there's no such thing as a wholly negative card in the Tarot. This is a painful picture, but look closer, for there's more hope here than you realize. This man has his back turned and if he would only turn around, he'd notice that two of his cups are still standing. Whatever his loss, it's very real and very painful. It isn't the end of the world, though, and he hasn't lost everything.

The two upright cups are on a road leading to a gateway filled with light and hope. What's your personal catastrophe? What have you lost or what's broken your heart? You've got a straightforward choice. You can move forward or you can carry on fixating on the spilt cups. That way you'll stand still and stagnate. Be upset and feel the pain by all means, but there will come a time when you have to move on for your own sake.

Choose to move on and you can salvage the two cups that remain. Follow the path to the brightly lit gateway and you'll discover that although life has some painful disappointments, there will be plenty more joys in the future. You may even find there are plenty more full cups further along the road.

Five is a number of difficulty and uncertainty. In the realm of the emotions, this can signify a very rocky process. Be brave and take stock. Life's dealt you a cruel blow here so let's not underestimate the pain. Let's not overestimate it, either. Draw on your inner strength and the support of friends to move forward. You're not beaten yet.

LOSS IN PLEASURE

$\mathcal{S}$ix cups float mysteriously on the water as the sun rises. A man watches birds fly over the waters, but his vision is clouded with hints of past remembrances and pleasures. Floating towards him is a postcard bearing the face of his former lover. The past has come back to haunt the present.

The *Golden Dawn* called this card "Pleasure," but it's much more than that. It's also about nostalgia and how the pleasures of the past can inform or haunt our present-day existence. In earlier traditions of fortune telling, this card would often signify the re-appearance of an old flame.

The number six often represents the concept of perfection, and in the suit of cups, this manifests as our idealizations of emotional perfection. How often have you looked back at a past relationship with rose-tinted glasses? It's too easy to look back nostalgically at a man we once loved and see only the good things that were shared. In the present, it can be too easy to look at a man we are attracted to and do something similar. We idealize him as the solution to all our needs and the fulfillment of all our desires. When we do this, the object of our affections turns from being a flesh and blood male to a false god.

It's dangerous to over idealize. When we set another man up on a pedestal like this we're not truly in love or showing love. We are merely worshipping an imaginary personification of our own desires. Real men have warts and all. They are difficult to love, not always easy to understand, and require genuine perseverance, sacrifice, and commitment if a relationship is going to work. In short, the bed of roses is in your dreams.

Why bother then, you may ask? Because the real thing, warts and all, with all the struggles and sacrifices you'll have to make, is infinitely more rewarding. What's really in your heart? Are you fruitlessly searching for the ideal of perfect pleasure in the form of a gleaming smile, square jaw, and a six pack? Have you set someone up in your heart as the solution to all your sadness? Maybe you're hoping that one special guy from the past will re-appear from nowhere and sweep you off your feet so you'll both live happily ever after. If that's the case, stop and take a long hard look at where you're going. Chances are it's a road to nowhere and you're missing the real golden opportunities for true and realistic happiness. A man who fulfills one hundred percent of your wishes is a myth, so stop looking. The man who only fulfills forty-five percent of your desires won't make you happy so don't sell yourself short. Somewhere out there is a man who ticks eight out of ten boxes. He's the one for you. You'll have enough in common to love each other deeply and to make it successful, but you'll be different enough to have to work at it. When we do this, we change and become more selfless.

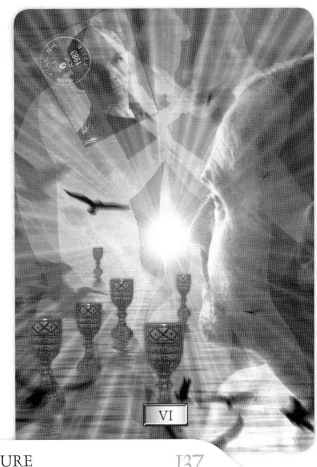

SIX OF CUPS

What do you really want out of life? Have you truly taken time out to ask yourself or are you reaching for every star you see, hoping that one of them might just bring you happiness? Just how greedy are you? Maybe you want it all at once and think you can have it now.

The Seven of Cups shows a man faced with a bewildering range of choices and visions. Above him, seven cups float within a full circular rainbow representing wholeness. From these cups swirl all his wildest dreams and desires and his visions hold him in a blissful state of powerlessness.

We can sometimes become so bound up in our dreams and aspirations that we lose our sense of reality. Wallowing in the hope of an ideal life, we fail to improve the one we already have. There are many visions within this card. A woman's face is framed with jewels, representing wealth. We also see a laurel wreath representing personal triumphs and a serpent to represent wisdom. A dragon shows the desire for the wondrous and the miraculous and a castle represents the man's desire for power and security.

We even see a beautiful man. Is he this man's ideal lover or is he a projection of the person he would like to be himself? We cannot tell as his face is hidden. Above all of these lurks the skull representing death. None of these visions or desires is bad in themselves, but for the man in the card, they are idealizations rather than realities. It's not wrong to dream of living in a castle, but for most of us, it's more realistic to be working towards an apartment or a house. There's nothing wrong in dreaming of personal triumphs as depicted by the wreath but again, just how realistic is your view of what you can achieve? You may dream of taking center stage in the opera, but maybe a place in the chorus is more realistic.

For some of us, one of these visions could be a realistic goal but others would still be out of reach. Wherever you stand, heed this card's message and keep your fantasies in check. Aspirations are good, but when they become unrealistic, the misguided quest to achieve them can prevent us from realizing our true destinies. None of us can have everything in life, but all of us can have something special. Know your limits.

Re-assess both what you want and what you need out of life and work towards realistic goals. Maybe you are clinging to unrealistic fantasies so you can avoid the true effort of working towards realistic achievements. Unrealistic expectations are ultimately empty and unfulfilling. When this card appears, it's time to re-assess where you're going and to set some realistic goals. Lessening your expectations may increase your inner and outer wealth.

SEVEN OF CUPS

VII

ILLUSIONARY SUCCESS

Have you ever struggled to feel happy within a friendship, relationship, workplace, or home that on the surface appears to be healthy? There comes a time when you just have to step back, walk away, or admit that despite all the effort you've put in, it just isn't working anymore. In theory, it's all there, but in practice, the situation's stagnant for everyone.

In the card, a naked man walks away from eight carefully arranged cups towards the rising sun. His nakedness is symbolic of his loss; he appears to be walking away with nothing. In the sky above him is a waning moon, signifying this particular phase is drawing to a close.

It's not as negative as it looks, however. The sunrise symbolizes a new chapter and a new beginning. There are times in life when walking away is the right thing to do. In a stagnant relationship, it's sometimes the case that both parties need to separate in order to grow and move forward. You may get back together but then again, you may not.

Where do you find yourself when you draw this card? When I designed it, I found myself needing to sell my house and re-locate to another part of the country. Leaving the cups behind symbolized my acceptance of the fact that my time in one place had come to a natural end. It was time to start a new life somewhere else in order to continue thriving.

It's difficult leaving that stack of cups behind when you've put so much effort into building them. Maybe work commitments draw you away to a new physical location heralding a new phase in your friendships or love life. Most painful of all, maybe you've tried everything to salvage a relationship gone sour or you've gone through traumas together that have changed you too much for the relationship to ever be the same again. The Eight of Cups is a sad but ultimately positive acknowledgment that it's time to move on.

Not all loves can be fixed once they've been broken. Not all loves are meant to be forever. If it's time to walk away, don't avoid the pain or the sadness. Grieve for what you're losing but cherish the special times you've had. Know also that this isn't simply the end. It's a new beginning.

ABANDONED SUCCESS 141

While the last few cards may have dealt with difficult issues and challenges, the Nine of Cups brings a more straightforward message – simply enjoy. Here, sky and water meet. Pink clouds blend seamlessly with blue waves whilst nine cups each contain their own splendid sun. Above them is a glowing pink triangle containing the smiling face of a man.

The gay community has a habit of turning other people's slurs into badges of triumph. The words "fairy," "faggot," and "queen," to name a few, have entered our vocabulary as part of our collective humor, despite their origins as terms of debasement in less tolerant days. Similarly, we have adopted former symbols of hatred as universal badges of triumph. There can be no more potent symbol of this than the pink triangle. The Nazis used this symbol on concentration camp uniforms to mark out homosexual prisoners, yet now our community has adopted it as a defiant badge of pride and remembrance. I love this symbol for its very existence in our midst bears witness to the power of love, bravery, and tolerance to overcome evil and hatred.

This card is a celebration of the openness and freedom we enjoy. It doesn't denote deep emotional fulfillment, but it encourages you to enjoy all the happiness that material pleasures can bring you. There are times in life just for enjoying transient pleasures. You may have a responsibility free period in your life when you can enjoy spending your hard-earned money without the encumbrance of mortgage or family expenditures. You may be free and single. If so, enjoy partying and the thrill of casual sex. None of these things can bring permanent happiness in their own right, but they certainly have their time and place. Enjoy the moment, for in their own measure, these can all bring a dose of emotional satisfaction.

Above all, next time life gifts you with one of these pleasures, remember who and what have gone before. Many men and women have made huge sacrifices in the past for the carefree happiness we enjoy today. In other less liberated parts of the world, brave men and women still make similar sacrifices which, in the future, will make their own countries better places for the likes of us. Enjoy the happiness of carefree and material pleasures. Considering the price paid for them by previous generations, they are to be treasured and celebrated. The pink triangle is a badge of happiness but it's also a badge of remembrance and respect.

VIIII

MATERIAL HAPPINESS

The heart of this card glows with a radiant sun that rises over healing waters – the perfect medium from which mature and perfected love can grow. We see a couple basking in these waters, and in their midst, is a tree representing the growth and stability of their relationship. Above them, ten cups hover within a rainbow.

Whereas the Nine of Cups represented transient happiness and lighthearted fulfillment, the Ten represents the depths and fulfillment of a mature same-sex relationship. This is a bond of love quite unlike anything we would ever experience between friends. These men have become soul mates to each other. They share a level of trust and intimacy that goes way beyond normal friendship. They have committed to each other and to no-one else. Their sexual union only serves to celebrate their love. They have eyes for no-one else.

This is the lifelong bond that many of us crave. In our partner, we somehow find our completion. Rather than losing ourselves, if the relationship is healthy and fulfilled, we find ourselves and we discover new flights of freedom.

How can you describe true love? It's too spectacular, complicated, and wonderful to sum up in a few words. One thing I do know is that you don't just find it on a plate. What these men share constitutes a lifetime's work. This kind of love only results when we choose to commit long term and work very hard to love and support one another.

Generally, the initial flames of lust and infatuation begin to subside in a relationship after a couple of years. That's when the real work begins. If you've made a wise and informed choice of partner, you begin to work together to fan the flames and keep them alive. You set aside special times for sex whereas before you would have been engaging in it spontaneously. You work hard to reconcile your differences, support each other, and above all, you work to love each other unconditionally.

Success in relationships isn't (as I've mentioned earlier) handed to anyone on a plate. As the *Golden Dawn's* name for this card suggests, deep level success and emotional fulfillment is perfected through hard work. Mutual respect, care, attention, and above all, unconditional love are the hallmarks of mature partnerships.

The hard work may be daunting but the rewards are sevenfold. I envy one of my oldest gay friends. He's now been with his partner for nearly eighteen years. In each other's eyes there can never be anyone else. Their sex life remains as passionate now as it was when they first met. They have separate bedrooms but build romantic games around who's room they will make love in tonight. When they need space to rest, the ritual of kissing good night and seeing each other safely to their respective spaces equally becomes an expression of love. They have supported each other through career changes, work stress, bereavements, family feuds, and a host of other trials. They have had their differences, and sometimes, I guess they have been tempted to walk away. Despite this, they love each other more now than they did when they first met. They have many friends, but there is that unique, special, and ultimately mystical place they reserve for each other. They are lovers; they are intimates. They are life partners.

When this card appears in a reading it speaks of destiny in the form of a soul mate. What are you looking for? Are you looking in the right places? Is this a vocation really for you? This is perfected love. Crafted over many years and bought at a high price, its rewards are uncountable.

TEN OF CUPS

THE CO

Our journey through the Major Arcana has shown us the higher realities of life. In visiting the Minor Arcana, we've seen snapshots of our everyday life experiences. Standing before the Court cards, we are brought face to face with real people; characters who reflect both ourselves and the personalities of those around us.

In the same tradition as playing cards, the Tarot depicts a series of Royal Courts, each ruling over one of the four kingdoms of the elements. A playing card suit will always contain three Court cards, whilst a standard Tarot deck suit contains four. Court figures can vary from deck to deck. Traditional decks such as the *Rider Waite* or the earlier *Marseilles* deck feature Kings, Queens, Knights, and Pages (Valets or Heralds) in their suits. More modern esoteric decks in the *Golden Dawn* or Crowley tradition replace the Knight and Page with the Prince and Princess.

In *The Son Tarot*, I've opted to make the courts wholly male. This does not exclude women from our readings; even in a traditional Tarot a court card can potentially symbolize either male or female, depending on the context. From a meditative view however, I've aimed for *The Son Tarot* courts to be an expression of both masculine and feminine qualities, but specifically as they express themselves through men. In these figures, we can celebrate all the essential attributes of each Court figure whilst maintaining and celebrating our masculine identity.

In each Court we see two authority figures and two figures of servitude. Rather than King and Queen, *The Son Tarot* features King and Prince, bound in same-sex marriage. The Court is completed by the Knight and the Herald who in their own ways convey the qualities of their respective suits. You could also say that the Knight and Herald represent modes of growth and learning, whilst the King and Prince are states of wisdom and experience.

THE COURT CARDS AS EXPRESSIONS
OF ELEMENTAL COMBINATIONS

The Tarot Courts show a reality where personality traits are defined by the various combinations of the four elements. Each suit has its primary elemental attribution, whilst each member of the Court brings a secondary elemental attribution into the mix. These combinations are set out in the table below.

For example, the Prince of Wands (Water of Fire) is where the empathy of emotion combines with the passion of creativity and sexuality. The fiery qualities of his libido flow out to others like a river.

As we explore each of these personality types, I'll examine them from the following different aspects:

CHARACTER/ CARD SUIT	KING (Fire - Libido)	PRINCE (Water - Heart)	KNIGHT (Air - Mind)	HERALD (Earth - Body)
Pentacles	Fire of Earth	Water of Earth	Air of Earth	Earth of Earth
Swords	Fire of Air	Water of Air	Air of Air	Earth of Air
Wands	Fire of Fire	Water of Fire	Air of Fire	Earth of Fire
Cups	Fire of Water	Water of Water	Air of Water	Earth of Water

AS AN ELEMENTAL FORCE

We'll look at how their individual combination of elements would manifest in the natural world and what that might symbolize within their personality types.

AS A ROLE MODEL

What kind of people would these figures practically manifest themselves as in our everyday lives?

AS A LOVER

If we encountered these figures specifically as men, lovers, and sexual partners, what would we experience and who would they be for us?

AS OURSELVES

How can we recognize these personality types within ourselves and embrace them whilst also recognizing their limitations and weaknesses?

AS A SHADOW CHARACTER

What is the dark side of this character. What is its reversal?

My hope is that you will begin to know these sixteen men, and in learning who they are, your readings will begin to make fuller sense. Lady Freida Harris, the famous Tarot artist who illustrated the Crowley *Thoth* deck, once described the Tarot as a:

"....CELESTIAL GAME OF CHESS, THE TRUMPS (MAJOR ARCANA) BEING THE PIECES TO BE MOVED ACCORDING TO THE LAW OF THEIR OWN ORDER OVER A CHECKERED BOARD OF THE FOUR ELEMENTS."

I would agree with Lady Freida whilst also seeing the Tarot on a more personal level. For me, the checkered board consists of the Major Arcana and numbered pips. The court cards are our chess pieces and as they move from square to square, the other cards become real life tableaux through which we see ourselves and those around us moving.

AS AN ELEMENTAL FORCE

The Herald of Pentacles is one of the four "pure" elemental cards, representing the essence of Earth itself. He also represents the potential for life that can spring from the soil, linking him to the traditional Tarot Empress and The Bountiful from *The Son Tarot* Major Arcana. Here we see life as it begins to manifest in the physical world. He represents the shooting of plants, the budding of leaves, and the unfurling of flowers. He is the herald of life itself.

AS A ROLE MODEL

Manifesting potential can be personified in two ways. Firstly, this man is a message bearer, bringing news of a birth. Whether a literal birth or not, his presence denotes that something has taken a new and substantive form in our lives. Manifesting potential can also be personified as an apprentice. Apprentices learn through doing, so the learning process and the manifestation of physical works are inseparable from each other.

AS A LOVER

The apprentice must also learn the physical ways of love. He is sexually inexperienced and possibly a virgin. He has all the wonders and joys of sex to discover, but must also learn that the physical skills of lovemaking are inextricably entwined with the emotions. He must be treated with care, nurture, and respect for if he gives you his intimacy, he is giving you the precious gift of his awakening. The simple innocence of such a man, whether he's a youth or someone only just coming out in later life, can be both a joy and a frustration. Let patience and compassion rule your heart, for despite his immaturity, this man can help you re-discover the youthful wonder of tasting a fruit you've yearned for so long.

AS OURSELVES

If we ourselves are only just discovering our sexuality, then this is our card. Even if we are long experienced, this card can denote the process of coming into our own bodies, learning to love ourselves and accepting ourselves as fully affirmed men. This is our potential to be a creative being, whether we are fashioning a great sculpture or simply building a wall in the garden. If we are learning with our hands then we are living this card.

AS A SHADOW CHARACTER

On a sexual level, this man goes out of control if his shadow side is exposed. He gives himself to promiscuity with little regard for the welfare of himself and others. On a practical level, the dark side of this herald shows an undisciplined, slapdash approach to learning new skills and a tarnished work ethic.

THE HERALD OF PENTACLES

HERALD OF PENTACLES

AS AN ELEMENTAL FORCE

This is the air that permeates down through the grains of the soil. It's the air generated by the countless millions of life forms that exist within the earth. Plants grow from the ground and as they photosynthesize they replenish our atmosphere with oxygen. Air of Earth can also be the rich reserves of gas locked deep within the rocks of the ground beneath us. As we draw on these riches we draw on the energy of the earth itself.

AS A ROLE MODEL

Earth is the least volatile of the elements, so this knight's behavior will reflect this. He does not readily ride out to battle, but he will steadfastly act as guardian for all that he loves, protects, and believes in. The gaseous reserves of the Earth are inert until touched by flame. Likewise, this knight is slow to be roused, but if his anger is ignited it will be furious. He isn't quick witted in his endeavors, but you will find him to be stolid and patient. Steady progress rather than fast results are his hallmark.

AS A LOVER

If you were to view any man as "your rock," this would be him. He may not be the most exciting, charming, or charismatic, but he will love and protect you to the last. His own aims and ambitions aren't necessarily his first priority, but he'll make yours his highest aim and give you the firmest platform from which to fly. Furthermore, he'll always be there when you return. You can be strong everywhere else because he gives you a safe place to be vulnerable when you're together. When you're in this man's arms, you feel nothing could ever harm you. If someone ever tried to do you harm, his reaction to protect you would be swift and terrible. He is a strong man, not to be trifled with.

AS OURSELVES

Whenever you selflessly step into the background to provide support and security for someone else, then you're fulfilling this role. Maybe you've sacrificed your own career development to support your partner's. Alternately, you could have given up work to care for someone you love who's seriously ill. Think of those strange accounts of mothers who find the raw strength to physically lift cars in order to free a trapped child. When someone we love is in mortal danger, we can be shocked by our own strength to save or protect them. Human beings have incredible reserves of energy for survival and this very volatility is the hallmark of the knight within us.

AS A SHADOW CHARACTER

Sloth is the shadow side of this man. He loses his motivation to act when necessary or he squanders his hidden energies in the wrong places. If care and compassion leave his heart he will turn to stone and never be roused.

THE KNIGHT OF PENTACLES

KNIGHT OF PENTACLES

AIR OF EARTH

153

AS AN ELEMENTAL FORCE

He is the water table. Dig deep enough into the ground and you'll find these hidden reserves of water contained in the earth. He also represents water within the soil, underground springs, and subterranean lakes. He is everything that makes the earth fertile.

AS A ROLE MODEL

This is a nurturing man. He's the sort of man who creates a safe space around others so that they can recuperate, regenerate and grow. He's acutely aware of the body and its needs and knows how to bring nourishment or refreshment. You often find people like this in caring professions such as nursing. People in need will often gravitate towards this kind of man as he will offer comfort and protection.

AS A LOVER

To lose yourself in this man's arms is a very safe place to be. He will comfort and cherish you and you'll always feel stronger for his embrace. In a relationship, he may often be the quieter and less conspicuous of the two parties, but he's invariably the stronger. Whilst you're out there working towards your goals, he'll be quietly behind you providing the strength and practical support you need. He's the secret garden and fountain of refreshment you'll always return to for replenishing your strength. When a man like this makes love to you, sexual intimacy becomes an act of healing in itself. Living with this man is like having a strong but gently protective pair of arms around you on a day by day basis.

AS OURSELVES

This is the healing and nurturing part of ourselves. Whenever we offer a combination of love and practical care, we are living this role. Love manifesting through practical support to a friend in need sets free the Prince of Pentacles within our hearts. The card shows his light and energy nurturing growth on the Earth; symbolically, this is our opportunity to put love to practical action.

AS A SHADOW CHARACTER

Rather than caring and nurturing through selfless love, this character can cause damage through neglect or malice. If turned inwards or evil, this man's nurturing capacity becomes deviously destructive but in a quiet, underhanded way. The shadow side of the Prince of Pentacles is someone who acts very much in the dark. He poisons relationships through backhanded gossip, then quietly slips into the background while others take the blame. He undermines confidence and withholds love. What he has to give will only be given conditionally, depending on your compliance to his desires. He's not the kind of abuser who will bulldoze your tower, but beware; he's the kind of man who slowly but surely burrows beneath the foundations and weakens them.

THE PRINCE OF PENTACLES

PRINCE OF PENTACLES

AS AN ELEMENTAL FORCE

He is the superheated molten rock beneath the earth's crust. The currents in this sea of lava cause continental plates to drift. Furthermore, this continental tug of war is the basic force behind earthquakes, tsunamis, and volcanic eruptions. The ferocity of the Earth is the domain of the King of Pentacles but we must also remember: This inner fire is one of the main reasons why the earth is a dynamic, living planet. On another level, you could see this king as the Green Man of pagan tradition. As the fire of earth, he is the life force of the earth itself and the lord of the forest.

AS A ROLE MODEL

The King of Pentacles is a powerful man whose influence underpins our lives, jobs and economy. Many would refer to him as a "mover" or "shaker." He is not the sort of King to change things by action or crusade. From a stable throne he pulls strings and exerts influence to bring about change. He is a patron figure, providing resources and support to uphold other people's work, business and growth. This king doesn't go out to his populace.

He holds court in his throne room and they come to him. Philanthropists are a good expression of this archetype.

AS A LOVER

This is a strong, supportive lover, one who you can very much look up to as a pillar of strength and stability. He is kind and gentle but never underestimate his gentleness or mistake it for weakness. It is ferocious strength held in restraint and the tenderness of his touch is the flipside of an iron fist. The magic of his lovemaking doesn't lie in dexterity or acrobatics, but in bonding with him, you are awakened to the very physicality of sex. You realize you are two spiritual flames contained within vessels of clay and you become aware of your connections to the rhythms of the Earth.

AS OURSELVES

Whenever we draw others close to ourselves in generosity we become the King of Pentacles. Even the simple act of sharing your table with friends is an act in his spirit. If people come to you in genuine need and you give generously, then you are mirroring his behavior. One aspect of parenthood is to provide an underlying financial security, allowing for your children's welfare and growth. This is another facet of the King. Similarly, we may use our resources to quietly underpin the welfare of our family, friends, partners, or community. Providing surrogate family security for our gay brothers and sisters can be a key aspect of fulfilling this role.

AS A SHADOW CHARACTER

Generosity gives way to restrictive control, and this character, if turning to the shadow side, can use his underlying influence to dominate and suppress. Power, wealth, and the control of others become like drugs to this character, and those trapped in his sphere will be prevented from reaching their full potential whilst living in fear. This dark King is a control freak who uses his supposed superiority and authority as a weapon of oppression.

THE KING OF PENTACLES

AS AN ELEMENTAL FORCE

He is matter carried within the atmosphere. He can be the great sand storms across the desert. He is also the atmospheric dust that colors both sunrise and sunset so spectacularly. If water solidifies into ice crystals in the upper atmosphere forming high clouds, these are also the domain of the Herald of Swords.

AS A ROLE MODEL

Crowley referred to this elemental combination as the materialization of ideas. On a practical level, this shows the Herald to be a student or researcher. His role is to gain wisdom through reasoning and analysis so rational thinking will hold more importance for him than the emotions or intuitive reasoning.

AS A LOVER

As always, the Herald represents a youthful state regardless of physical age. This is a man beginning his quest for knowledge and understanding. Such men make challenging lovers as it is difficult for them to submit to the moment without resorting to introspection. A man like this will think a lot about "feeling" but finds it difficult to "feel" un-selfconsciously. He is like a spectator to his own emotions and will find it a challenge to directly experience his lover's emotional energy.

AS OURSELVES

Despite the drawbacks of this personality where intimate relationships are concerned, his strength is his ability to detach where necessary. We experience the positive side of this character whenever we become able to step aside from our troubles and see our circumstances objectively enough to formulate solutions. The Herald of Swords symbolizes our essential ability to fly high above confusion.

AS A SHADOW CHARACTER

Dust in the atmosphere can also act to conceal light from the sun. On the same level, the dark side of this character is his ability to veil the truth. Swords are a weapon and this man can cause strife and division through a combination of deception and concealment. If he turns dark, his analytical ability becomes twisted towards manipulation and malicious gossip. He is dangerous enough to set a stage of confusion, then quietly step into the background as those he has manipulated cause damage to each other.

THE HERALD OF SWORDS

HERALD OF SWORDS

AS AN ELEMENTAL FORCE

As one of the four "pure" elemental Court cards, he is the pure nature of air itself. This could be a breeze to refresh on one hand or the blast of a hurricane bringing destruction on the other.

AS A ROLE MODEL

Pure air symbolizes purity of mind and intellect. He is the archetypal champion, both of thought and valor. On an intellectual level, this character could manifest as the scientist making great breakthroughs or discoveries. On a heroic level, this is a champion who storms to victory on his charger. Unlike the Knight of Pentacles who stolidly protects what he cherishes, this knight will actively ride out to fight for his beliefs. His compassion is as great as his anger is terrible.

AS A LOVER

It is no understatement to say that this is the archetypal "knight in shining armor." If you're in love with a man like this, it's usually based on a certain amount of hero worship. He's a lover to look up to as a tower of strength. His love for you will be ferocious and he would go to the ends of the earth to protect you. If you're with a man like this, you'll never be alone in crisis; he'll be there to support you every step of the way whilst fighting your corner. There are times when his intensity can seem a little cold and you'll wonder what's going on in his head. Physically, if you like your lovemaking wild and untamable, then this is your man. On every level his power and swiftness are difficult to resist.

AS OURSELVES

This man is within all of us, if only we can be brave enough to tap into his energies. He represents all our hidden reserves of valor and our personal crusades for justice and honesty. Whenever we are convicted of our own inner strength and believe in our ability to win out for what is right, then we experience the essence of this knight.

AS A SHADOW CHARACTER

When this character turns to the dark side, justice is abandoned and his ferocious strength turns to a cold ruthlessness. This is a man who no longer cares for the just causes of others. His fight is only for selfish ends and he doesn't care who gets hurt in the process. His only priority is himself.

THE KNIGHT OF SWORDS

AIR OF AIR

AS AN ELEMENTAL FORCE

He is symbolized by rain, snow, water vapor, and storm clouds. Water in the atmosphere is a conductor of electricity, so this prince is also represented by lightning in its various forms.

AS A ROLE MODEL

Dark clouds, rainstorms, and lightning all symbolize upheaval. Ally these to the divisive nature of the sword and we begin to see this prince as the archetypal divorcee or a man who has been widowed. He knows only too well the anguish of a broken relationship, and through much soul searching, he has come to understand both his former lover's mistakes and his own short comings. Bitter experience has taught him not to suffer fools gladly. Honesty is paramount to him and he will not tolerate insincerity or compromise. He speaks the truth bluntly and calls hypocrisy by its name. A single word from this man has the power to cut through a thousand lies.

AS A LOVER

It's difficult to win this man's trust as a lover. After all, he's been hurt in the past and it takes time before he'll lower his protective mask for you. When he does, he'll bring both wisdom and maturity to your relationship. He understands the pain of loss or relationship breakdown and has matured through the process. He takes nothing about you or your love for one another for granted, for he knows just how easily it can all evaporate. You can only win this man's trust in love if you're prepared to be open and transparent to him. If you gave him anything less, he would see right through it. He can read you like a book, and on one level, it's comforting to be known so deeply. On another level, there's nowhere to hide from a man like this and it's a challenge to be constantly drawn on to higher levels of truthfulness.

AS OURSELVES

The Prince of Swords represents our ability to deal maturely with rejection. The pain of separation is something we all experience throughout our lives. This may not be due to the breakdown of a romantic relationship; it could also be connected with conflicts of friendship, strife in our workplace, or even to a family bereavement. We can only grieve such losses and move forward. Hopefully, we can be open enough to allow our wisdom to be enriched along the way.

AS A SHADOW CHARACTER

The dark side of this man is someone who has turned bitter as a result of his personal losses. He is crippled by repressed anger and refuses to move on, failing to forge new connections or relationships. He is swift to criticize others yet will not accept criticism concerning his own behavior.

THE PRINCE OF SWORDS

PRINCE OF SWORDS

AS AN ELEMENTAL FORCE

The King of Swords represents the raw power of wind and storm. The weather systems of our atmosphere are fueled by the heat of the sun and it's this very combination of heat and volatile air that he personifies. You could also say that the King is the fiery atmosphere of the sun itself. As the solar wind flares out across the Solar System its influence is felt to a greater or lesser extent by each of the planets, even furthest one. On Earth, our planet's magnetic field deflects the solar winds to the poles and we experience them as the Technicolor display of the Aurora Borealis.

AS A ROLE MODEL

Air is the element of reason, balance, and Justice. When fueled by fire, these qualities become impassioned and we see a person who rules from the heart and lives for all that is honest or good. Social justice and equality are key issues for this man, and while in a position of authority, he will not tolerate unfairness. He's the sort of man who lives by the maxim of an honest day's pay for an honest day's work and he doesn't tolerate oppression or bullying within his sphere. The biblical story of King Solomon passing judgment over two women who both claimed motherhood of a single baby illustrates this character well. To trick the untruthful of the two claimants, Solomon decreed that the baby should be cut in half, giving each woman a fair share. He knew full well that the real mother would reveal herself by renouncing her claim in favor of the other to protect her child. This she duly did and the King saw the baby rightfully returned to her. His judgments are often uncompromising, but they will always be rooted in fairness.

AS A LOVER

This is a tough man to be in a relationship with as he demands the best from himself, from you, and from others. This is why you love him. His compassion and integrity are two of his most admirable qualities and his influence will draw you to new heights you haven't dreamt of. Above all, this man inspires you with his integrity and moves your conscience. Being with him makes you see the world in a whole new way; your focus shifts from yourself to the needs of others and you begin to see life in terms of what you can give rather than what you receive.

AS OURSELVES

This man represents our deepest social conscience. Whenever we help a friend in need, contribute to the building of the community or fight against a social injustice, then we are embodying the King of Swords. The card itself shows suggestions of swords of truth, scales of justice, and two figures that could be bound together in unity or dispute. Behind them, all is the face of the King, crowned by a butterfly; the symbol of emerging freedom. The King is our conscience in union with our passions. Whenever we act for justice in a heartfelt manner, we enable freedom for ourselves and others.

AS A SHADOW CHARACTER

The fiery blast of the storm can only destroy when the dark side of a man like this emerges. He is as willful as ever but the quest for justice has been replaced by a selfish quest for self-interest. As a ruler, this man becomes a tyrant or a dictator.

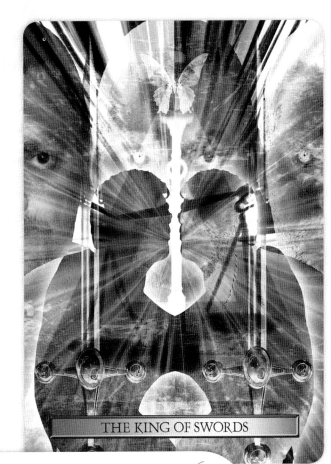

THE KING OF SWORDS

FIRE OF AIR

AS AN ELEMENTAL FORCE

Here is the origin of fire. The Herald of Wands symbolizes all on the earth that will ignite and combust. He is fossil fuel. He is firewood. He is the blue touch paper to be lit on a firework.

AS A ROLE MODEL

This is someone who contains childlike energy within themselves. Someone like this views the world with an almost innocent wonder. Their inner fire is bright and filled with an enthusiasm for life. Never simplistic, but always straightforward, knowing someone like this helps to restore our childlike faith in the essential goodness of being alive. They bring with them new hope, new ideas, and above all, fresh energy and a willingness to take risks. Great potential for creativity is contained within the heart of someone like this. It must simply be nurtured and encouraged by those around him.

AS A LOVER

Slightly fumbling, somewhat innocent but passionate and fervent in the ways of love. A man like this may not have many sexual wiles and he certainly doesn't have great sexual experience but his youthful energy will sweep you up, regardless of his physical age. This is a man discovering the potent energy of his sexuality and open to exploration. He will look to you to be his guide and will reward you richly for taking the lead. Delight with him as he delights in the discovery of his own body, his inner fires and the pleasure they can give him. As he grows, he must learn to steward his sexual energy wisely, maintaining a healthy balance between sexual gratification and spiritual equilibrium. For now, he understands little of how his sexuality and spirituality are linked.

AS OURSELVES

Whenever we are in need of spiritual, creative, work or sexual guidance, we become the Herald of Wands. He is the part of us that remains forever young and whatever levels of maturity we reach, we must always maintain enough humility to understand there will always be others wiser than ourselves. We must also recognize our own potential to bring transformation, be it to other people or to the environment around us. Wherever we go we carry this potential with us. It is for others to light the blue touch paper should they choose to.

AS A SHADOW CHARACTER

If this character is darkened, his childlike wonder and openness becomes a stubborn refusal to grow up and take responsibility. In this man's eyes, it's always someone else's fault when something goes wrong and he will not take responsibility for the damage he causes to others.

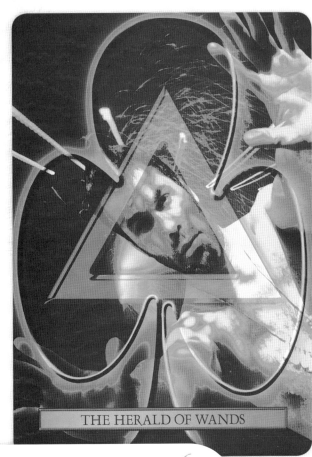

THE HERALD OF WANDS

HERALD OF WANDS

EARTH OF FIRE

AS AN ELEMENTAL FORCE

Billowing smoke, flammable gases, and the rush of flames denote the Knight of Wands. He is a raging fire fanned by the winds.

AS A ROLE MODEL

This man storms in and transforms everything in his wake. In a business setting, he can be the maverick operator who transforms and restores an ailing company. On an artistic level, he takes inspiration to new heights and infects those around him with new levels of creativity. The card shows him crowned with a radioactivity "danger" symbol. Change is a very dangerous thing. Are you truly ready for the fiery passion and winds of transformative change this man can bring?

AS A LOVER

Sex with a man like this is something akin to the fastest and most extreme rollercoaster ride you can imagine. He's a devastatingly accomplished lover and you'll be both overpowered and swept up by his sexual prowess at the same time. This man may not have the depths of emotion and spirituality you would find in the Prince of Wands, but for sheer thrills and intensity no lover can match him. His intelligence and libido go hand in hand, and without you realizing, he's analyzed your behavior, body language, and personality with a view to matching his sexual behavior to your desires. He seems to know instinctively what it is that turns you on and he's there before you even ask.

AS OURSELVES

The Knight of Wands is our own potential to change and transform our surroundings and the people around us. We are not merely passive spectators in our jobs or personal lives. We all have a rich contribution to make, and to a great extent, the world around us is what we are prepared to make of it. He is also our capacity to be creative and playful in our works. Both life and sex benefit from his injection of carefree joy.

AS A SHADOW CHARACTER

When this character turns sour, his capacity to sweep in with positive change becomes confrontational and war like. His motives become ego driven and his actions promote conflict, disharmony, and resentment. The motivator becomes the task master and this man's workforce will feel both constricted and repressed. On a physical level, sex becomes a means to an end – a means of satisfying his own needs with no care for others. Such a man leaves his lovers feeling used or degraded.

THE KNIGHT OF WANDS

KNIGHT OF WANDS

AS AN ELEMENTAL FORCE

As water of fire, he represents fire in fluid motion. This is a river of molten lava or any other way that fire flows across the earth.

AS A ROLE MODEL

This is someone from whom there is a constant flow of sacred, sexual, and creative energy. They are deeply connected to the unseen spiritual world around them. Fire touches, knows, and transforms, so this man has a deep talent for understanding the inner lives of both himself and others. It's difficult not to feel the influence of someone like this as their very presence in your life has a profound effect. This man has uncanny spiritual and personal discernment; you'll be amazed at how well he can see through you and into you. The card image shows him with a visible third eye connected with his base chakra, for his vision and his passions are different manifestations of the same energy.

AS A LOVER

Crowley connected the Queen of Wands to the mysteries of Bacchus. As her counterpart in this deck, the Prince is certainly a fount of sexual energy. He understands his own body to a very deep level and spontaneously channels the full power of his libido so as to engulf you in ecstasy when you make love. Sex with a man like this is akin to a whirlpool of sexual energy. You are both engulfed and ignited at the same time. More than any other man in the Tarot court, sex is a powerful means of forging emotional connection and a pathway to higher spiritual truth. Both earth and sky move when you make love to a man like this. Can you be brave enough to be swept along?

AS OURSELVES

He is the hidden fire within all of us. The practice of Tantra as a discipline is one of the ways to unlock the sexual power of the Prince of Wands within us. Meditation or divination can similarly begin to unlock the potential of his second sight. We enact this man's energy when sex becomes a connection of both body and spirit. His way is perilous as to follow him is to both know and to be known. Are you ready?

AS A SHADOW CHARACTER

Truth, passion, and knowledge give way to sexual abandon, license, and depravity when this character is darkened. His spiritual powers are either neglected or misused to the detriment of others. Here is the world of the fake psychic who pedals his trade for financial gain or someone who misuses spiritual gifts for self-promotion. Sexual addiction or promiscuity with no spiritual and emotional balances are also part of this darkened character.

THE PRINCE OF WANDS

PRINCE OF WANDS

AS AN ELEMENTAL FORCE

One of the four "pure element" cards, he is the essence of fire itself. He is flame, light, heat, and plasma. As a living flame, he is matter in flux and transformation.

AS A ROLE MODEL

As the essence and master of the creative force, this man usually manifests as an authority figure or a spiritual elder. In the work place, this can be a manager or chief executive with years of work experience, wisdom, and authority behind him. He is a gold mine of experience and someone who you can always turn to for guidance and sound advice. Spiritually, this would be the elder of the tribe or a spiritual leader. Again, his wisdom is founded in solid experience and he guides his charges with quiet authority and humility. In the creative realm, think of this man as one of the great masters with a school of artistic apprentices under him. The Leonardos and Michaelangelos of this world, along with great composers such as Bach, Mozart, and Beethoven have fulfilled this role.

AS A LOVER

This man isn't just your lover. He becomes your guide, your authority figure, and your protector, too. Your attraction to him lies not only in his inner and outer beauty, but also in his deeds, and looking up to this man forms a large part of your love and devotion. Fire is fire; it purifies all that it touches, meaning that this man has a natural honesty that demands transparency in return. Your love making is fiery and passionate but it's also well-nigh impossible to hide anything in your intimacy. Physicality with this man goes hand in hand with honesty in relating and a healthy sex life is maintained in tandem with emotional openness.

AS OURSELVES

Age and experience bring wisdom. Whether we lose our outer beauty as we grow older is a matter for debate, but we certainly gain positively on the inside. We grow in experience and find ourselves passing on that wisdom to those in our charge. Wherever we find ourselves in a position of seniority or authority, we can potentially fulfill the role of the King of Wands. His place is to guide and encourage whilst letting those in his charge fulfill their full potential and find their destiny.

AS A SHADOW CHARACTER

In his healthy aspect, the King of Wands guides and encourages whilst allowing the freedom for you to grow. He advises, but ultimately, you must choose your own path. By contrast, the shadow side of the King becomes domineering and controlling; he is a dictator that will only tolerate his way and no other. His fire becomes a tool of repression instead of a force for transformation.

THE KING OF WANDS

KING OF WANDS

FIRE OF FIRE

AS AN ELEMENTAL FORCE

He symbolizes the sediment in seas and rivers. Rivers carve their way through the landscape, eroding the ground beneath them and carrying great weights of minerals and nutrients to new locations. Likewise, the sea is enriched with sand and sediments churned up from its own bed and from the rivers that flow into it. Earth of Water is all the material riches carried along by water's ebb and flow and the Herald of Cups symbolizes someone who has the potential to nourish us on so many different levels as we connect ourselves to his heart. He also symbolizes the fact that the emotional and the physical world are inextricably intertwined, particularly where our bodies are concerned.

AS A ROLE MODEL

As the symbolic youth figure of the court, the Herald of Cups represents an adolescent, a youth or someone only just emerging into emotional maturity. He gazes in wonder down into his cup for it contains the emerging secrets of his emotional life and his personal growth. This figure can also be a fully grown man, particularly if he's only

just coming out. Men like these are sometimes just beginning to learn the arts of relating and of forging emotional bonds. They are experiencing that rite of passage that others would have traveled much earlier on in their lives. As such they need patient nurturing and a little protection from those around them.

AS A LOVER

This is a young lover, often inexperienced, yet filled with the wonder of discovering the joys of romance and the profundity of knowing/being known. His combination of innocence and intensity can be overwhelming on one hand, but enriching on the other. Making love to a man like this, whether he's young or old, helps us to remember and reconnect with the freshness of first love. It's sometimes difficult to keep the Herald of Cups on track as he's only just finding his emotional feet, but he has the power to make us feel inwardly young again. A note of caution sounds only to say that balance must be continually maintained. Intimacy with a man like this could easily spill over into caretaking his immaturity whilst forgetting your own needs.

AS OURSELVES

He is our own inner youth as seen through the flow of our emotions. Remember how you felt when you were first in love and you'll rediscover the Herald of Cups within yourself. He is also a symbol of how our emotional lives affect our physical well-being. Look to your body. Are your levels of emotional well-being enhancing or adversely affecting your physical health?

AS A SHADOW CHARACTER

This is someone who refuses to take responsibility for their own emotional behavior. They can potentially leave much damage in their wake and they remain unwilling to face the challenge of growing up emotionally and taking responsibility for others as well as themselves.

THE HERALD OF CUPS

EARTH OF WATER

AS AN ELEMENTAL FORCE

The airy part of water is steam and water vapor, so the Knight of Cups is akin to a surging cloud or to bubbling water. He is the volatility of our emotions. He is our dreams and our unbridled passions. If water is the symbol of the emotions, then here we see them bursting forth energetically rather than flowing steadily.

AS A ROLE MODEL

The Knight of Cups is the archetypal dreamer or romantic lover. His desire is to love to the full and to experience every range of emotional joy the heart has to offer. He follows his heart with total conviction and will always dare to dream high whether it's in love or in attainment. He believes fully in the power of love as a road to fulfillment. Despite all of this, he also has the power to bring his rational mind to bear on his heart. If needs be, he can adopt a practical and level headed attitude, bringing gravity to a relationship where necessary.

AS A LOVER

This man will sweep you off your feet. He'll carry you up in a surge of romantic feeling and lay his heart at your feet. To be loved by such a man is almost to be worshipped, yet you'll also find he has the cool-headed ability to be practical. He lives for love, but he's wise enough not to let emotion stand in the way of practicality when necessary. This man can learn to be practical in whatever way necessary to see a relationship forward.

AS OURSELVES

The Knight of Cups is a symbol of our own capacity to aim high with our dreams. Air and water in this combination allow us to channel our desires freely whilst wisely taking stock of how best to achieve them. Likewise in our relationships, he represents the ability to be passionate without being impractical.

AS A SHADOW CHARACTER

He becomes an unscrupulous seducer. When integrity is taken away, this man will use his romantic wiles for his own gain, be it for sex or money. His clear-headed rationale remains, but the warmth of his heart is absent, leading to a lack of concern for others' welfare. He will tell you he loves you today but he will be gone tomorrow.

THE KNIGHT OF CUPS

AIR OF WATER

AS AN ELEMENTAL FORCE

The Prince of Cups is one of the four "pure" elemental manifestations within the Court cards. He represents the depths of the oceans and the deep-sea currents. Symbolically, this represents the deepest stirrings of our hearts. Here is a man who is eminently in touch with the depths of human feeling and the workings of the heart, both in himself and in others.

AS A ROLE MODEL

This man is an empath. He doesn't reason so much as he feels. He may not be able to tell you why he understands something, but you'll discover his understanding is uncannily accurate, particularly where people are concerned. This is a man who connects wholeheartedly. Life for him is not to be lived in isolation; he defines his life by the emotional connections he makes and the nourishment that flows to and fro through them.

AS A LOVER

If this man holds you close, you'll lose yourself in his eyes. If you look deep enough, you'll begin to see those eyes hold your reflection. To be with a man like this is to know and be known and connecting with him teaches you what it means for two to become one. The card shows his face tattooed with a heart. He floats within an ocean of feelings from which emerges a representation of the Kabbalistic tree of life. Just as the spheres of the tree are interconnected, so is his heart interconnected with those of all around him.

AS OURSELVES

The Prince of Cups is our ability to experience our emotions freely and to understand them. He represents our ability to reach out to and connect with others in a compassionate way.

AS A SHADOW CHARACTER

This personality becomes dishonest, unstable and emotionally dependent. He can be overly clingy and manipulative in an underhanded way. A stalker or someone neurotically possessive can be the more extreme manifestations of this shadow character.

THE PRINCE OF CUPS

WATER OF WATER

AS AN ELEMENTAL FORCE

Imagine water bubbling up from the ocean's depth, heated by the eruption of deep-sea volcanoes. Imagine the sheer sun-generated energy that drives the ocean currents and causes waves to thunder and crash. This is the King of Cups and these elemental energies symbolize love in powerful motion. This goes beyond mere romantic love and feelings; this is the overwhelming fire of charity and compassion. This is love driven to act because he is love fueled by passion.

AS A ROLE MODEL

This is a person who loves unconditionally. He is the ultimate ruler of the kingdom of the emotions and his heart gives freely and sensibly to those who are in need. Sometimes his capacity to give seems overwhelming. One wonders when his reserves of selflessness will be exhausted because they never seem to be. His generosity and compassion can sometimes move us to tears.

AS A LOVER

In the arms of such a man we feel safe for life. This partner will love you and cherish you until death do you part. He accepts you for who you are and nothing else. All the things that make you who you are become the very reasons he loves you. In his eyes, even your faults are part of his treasure. In the intimacies of lovemaking he will be like a tidal wave that sweeps you up, because for him, sex is a powerful means of channeling his feelings of love.

AS OURSELVES

We see this king within ourselves whenever our emotions are stoked by the flames of our passions. His energy within us moves us to love unconditionally and causes us to look beyond ourselves for the welfare of others. If we are moved to care for those in desperate need or to do charitable work, we are living this personal archetype.

AS A SHADOW CHARACTER

In vengeance, this man uses his inner fire to wreak revenge or hatred in the emotional realm. He can be emotionally controlling or domineering. Domestic violence also falls into the dark territory of the shadow side of this king. Wherever love becomes conditional or where it is replaced with bitterness, this king's light is lost.

THE KING OF CUPS

FIRE OF WATER

WORKING

INTRODUCTION

Now that you've completed your journey through the cards, it's time to make them work for you. This isn't just about learning the various techniques of card reading; it's also about making the cards your own.

The meanings given for each card in this book are my interpretations based on my own life experience. It is my hope that they act as a guide and an introduction, but what matters most are your own experiences and the response of your heart to these images. If you read my written descriptions and resonate with them, it's wonderful, but I'd encourage you to begin attaching your own personal meanings and significances to the cards as well.

Everyone has a unique and individual life path. Your experiences and the very way you view life will be different from mine and from everyone else's. When you step into the drama of each of these cards, you will inevitably bring something of your own to each scenario. Taking the Six of Wands as an example, my response to that card would be very different to that of a professional gay athlete or army officer. The basic message of the card is universal but our differing life experiences lead to a different range of responses, feelings, and aspirations. I've written at length about mine. Now it's time to discover yours.

The first exercises included here are meditative and aim to take you deeper into the card images themselves. There are also some "storytelling" exercises where you can use the cards as a tool for clarifying how you see your own experiences and aspirations. The final exercises show you how to perform readings using a selection of different card spreads, each designed with varying questions or circumstances in mind.

VISUALIZATION WITH THE CARDS

VISUALIZATION EXERCISE NUMBER 1

STEPPING INTO A CARD IMAGE.

The aim here is to help you forge a personal connection with each of the card images. Make a quiet and undisturbed space for yourself. Sit yourself comfortably, relax and clear your mind of any anxieties or distractions. Once you feel grounded, select the card that you feel the most drawn to at that given moment. Hold it in your hand and focus on the image in order for you to enter its world.

When you feel ready, close your eyes and imagine the image as a life-size door before you. In your mind's eye, step through and enter that world. How does it make you feel? Are you glad to be in this particular place? How do you respond to the people you meet there? What do you want to say to them and equally, if they speak, what are they saying to you?

Most of the images in *The Son Tarot* are very multi-layered and surreal. When I do this exercise myself, I envisage their landscapes in the same way I would see a surreal animation or something out of a pop video. If something looks disembodied, surreal or transparent in the card, go with it and let it be the same in your vision. The cards take us into the realm of dreams and the subconscious. Where the constraints of reality are removed, so also are the constraints of possibility. You are real but you're about to enter a world of fantasy. Let your imagination run wild and let it teach you a thing or two as it does.

MY JOURNEY THROUGH THE TEN OF SWORDS.

I step into this image and find myself standing on the water as if it's a glass floor. I see the blood of the dead man seeping through the water and it fills me with horror and sadness. There's nothing I can do for him. I know I must journey towards the other nine swords in the sunrise. They are somehow my destiny but I feel small, insignificant, and overwhelmed by how far away they are. As I walk, I grow bigger and my steps grow wider. I reach the swords faster than I could have thought. I now tower over them rather than having to look up and I am strong enough to draw the largest sword out of the water. I raise it in triumph. I look back along my path to discover the dead man has gone and the water is clear. In his place is someone living and he too holds a sword, the tenth sword in his hands, raising it in triumph. It is the one that used to pierce his heart.

VISUALIZATION EXERCISE NUMBER 2

A MAN STEPS OUT THE CARD AND INTO YOUR ROOM.

Stand the card of your choice on a mantelpiece, altar, or table and prepare yourself for your visionary journey in the same way mentioned for the previous exercise. Close your eyes and imagine the card growing into a life-size doorway. Through that door and into your room steps the key character from the card. He has a message for you. What is that message and what will you say to him before he steps back through the doorway and closes it? Receive his message, thank him, tell him what you need to say, and wish him a safe journey as he travels back into the card. Close the door behind him, and again, in your mind's eye, watch the card shrink back to its normal size. Open your eyes and take stock of your vision.

MY MEETING WITH THE MAN FROM THE SIX OF CUPS.

When I performed this visualization with the Six of Cups, the man didn't actually step out of the image. He saw me looking at the flying postcard and seemed to understand who I saw on the photograph. He just turned to me, looked, and said,

"I know. I miss him too."

VISUALIZATION EXERCISE NUMBER 3

BECOME THE MAN IN THE CARD.

Own the card in the most personal way possible. Again, having prepared yourself as mentioned previously, step into the card and become the character of your choice. Don't limit yourself to the characters you're drawn to or admire. Do the same with the ones you dislike or feel uneasy with. How do you feel about being this person? How do you feel about the actions you're performing? Do you feel up to your role or are you overwhelmed?

MY EXPERIENCE OF "BECOMING" JUSTICE.

I stepped into the Justice card and took my place. I immediately felt uncomfortable and constricted. I'd become a pillar, rooted deep in the earth. Nothing could shake me. I had the stability to weigh all the issues of life on my scales, yet I felt constricted and unable to move. I was overwhelmed with the responsibility of the choices that were mine to make and the scales felt heavy, yet there was an inner light and fire beginning to burn within me. This was the eternal law of justice and I somehow knew that, as a force buried within me, it would help me to weigh the scales accurately. Being this man was interesting, but uncomfortable. I wasn't at ease with the magnitude of the judgments I had to make and I was happy to relinquish my role. It left me with increased admiration for those who take on this role in real life.

TELL YOUR STORY WITH THE CARDS

Sometimes it helps to recount the narrative of what we've been through so we can understand ourselves more effectively. In telling the tale, we work through its impact on ourselves and formulate new ways of moving forward. When words don't come easily, pictures can often fill the gap. This is where you can use the card images to build a narrative.

Choose a selection of cards that you feel best illustrate the key points of your story. Lay them out chronologically, starting with the beginning of your account on the left and ending with the concluding card on the right. Also select a number of cards to identify the feelings you've gone through as you've made this journey. Dot them above and below the main row of cards, placing them on the sequence where you feel you experienced those emotions. If other people played a role in your story, use Court cards to illustrate them. Finally, draw some concluding cards; one to illustrate how you feel the situation has ended, another to show its effect on you, and a final card to show where you would ideally want to be.

With this exercise, it's often constructive to write down your thoughts as you're working through each card. It can also be a good thing to attempt to re-tell your story from an outsider's point of view, just using the cards themselves as your guide. Compare the two versions of the story – your own subjective one and the second more detached version spelled out by the card images alone. How do they fit together and what do they say about each other?

At all times use your own intuitive interpretations of the card images alongside the explanations given in this book. You may choose to abandon the written meanings altogether and just go with your own subjective responses to the images. This is equally valid. What matters most is that you feel the images accurately reflect your feelings about the story being told.

SHARING WITH THE CARDS

SHARING EXERCISE NUMBER 1

HOW DO WE SEE EACH OTHER?

Do this exercise with your partner, a friend, or in a group of friends. Spread your cards out on the floor and draw cards for each other, picking the card that you best feel describes your friend the most accurately. This can be a Court card to illustrate their personality, but it could equally be a Major Arcana to denote one of their deeper qualities, or simply a pip card to show what you see them going through at this given time.

A variation on this exercise is to choose two cards, one for strengths and a second for weaknesses. Explain your choices to one another and help each other to see how other people see you. Most importantly, do this in a way that affirms the value of your friends and builds people up in a sense of trust.

SHARING EXERCISE NUMBER 2

TELL PEOPLE HOW YOU SEE YOURSELF.

Within your couple or your group of friends, choose the card that you feel best illustrates yourself. Share your choices with each other and talk through why this choice of card is so personal to you. You may learn a lot about each other.

SHARING EXERCISE NUMBER 3

SPIRITUAL AND LIFE MAPPING IN GROUPS.

The method is the same as used for telling your own story with the cards as mentioned earlier. Here, you're mapping out your spiritual or life journey to date, so you can share your stories with each other. Photocopy your cards so you can stick the copies onto a large sheet of paper. Join them up with arrows and make notes on the chart to illustrate your story. This chart becomes the map of your journey. You may want to continue the map into the future, adding to it as you go or sticking on cards that illustrate where you would like to be.

192

CARD READING

Shuffle the deck thoroughly before drawing your cards. My own preferred method is to shuffle the cards then fan them out face down in a row so that I can make my selection at random. Focus lightly on your question as you select the relevant number of cards and let your intuition guide your hands. There are countless different ways to lay out the cards, depending on the nature of your question. When you're confident with the cards, you can even formulate your own. In the meantime, there are numerous books devoted purely to Tarot spreads if you wish to explore further. I'm including some of my favorites here. These are spreads I use regularly. They are also ideal for anyone new coming to card reading.

Remember, when reading the Tarot, it's not about a fixed picture of the future. Tarot is about possibilities and how you deal with them. Tarot is a game of "what if's" and the greatest learning comes from being honest about how we feel about the various possibilities before us.

THE CELTIC CROSS SPREAD

This is the most traditional and widely used of Tarot spreads. It's also one of the most versatile and ideal when you're looking for a good general overview of what's going on. The spread includes ten cards. Lay them out in the sequence shown in the diagram.

CARD 1: THE PRESENT CIRCUMSTANCES.

Whatever your question, this denotes where things are now.

CARD 2: THE CROSSING CARD.

This shows any factors that directly affect the present or interfere with it.

CARD 3: THE CROWN.

This shows the best that can be achieved through your circumstances. Alternately, it denotes any over-arching influences over your situation.

CARD 4: THE ROOT.

The distant past or whatever's at the root of your situation.

CARD 5: THE RECENT PAST.

Whatever's set the scene for where you're at.

CARD 6: THE NEAR FUTURE.

Factors to bear in mind when looking at what's to come.

CARD 7: YOURSELF.

How you fit into the present circumstances.

CARD 8: ENVIRONMENT.

Your surroundings or the circles you're moving in.

CARD 9: THE DOUBLE EDGED SWORD.

Your hopes and/or fears.

CARD 10: RESOLUTION.

The potential outcome.

Celtic Cross

THE SIX-CARD CHALLENGE SPREAD

I use this short spread as a simple way to explore my present circumstances and the potential challenges I may face.

CARD 1: THE PRESENT.

CARD 2: MY CHALLENGE.

CARD 3: ADVICE FOR FACING MY CHALLENGES.

CARD 4: A POTENTIAL RESOLUTION FOR MY CHALLENGE.

CARD 5: ENCOURAGEMENT FOR MY JOURNEY.

CARD 6: PROPHECY. A POSSIBLE OUTCOME TO CONSIDER.

6 Card Challenge

THE THREE-CARD SPREAD

This is the simplest of spreads and ideal for gaining a quick overview of how you see any given situation.

CARD 1: THE PAST AND HOW I SEE IT.

CARD 2: THE PRESENT AND HOW I SEE IT.

CARD 3: THE FUTURE, MY HOPES AND MY FEARS.

3 Card Spread

A FINAL WORD

A FINAL WORD

IF YOU'VE COME this far, this is only the beginning. I wish you a safe and prosperous journey as you explore the world of the cards. The further you travel, the more you'll understand just how far you still have to go. The language of the Tarot is a treasure chest of hundreds of years of accumulated wisdom. You could spend a lifetime just scratching the surface of that wisdom. Maybe that's the fun and joy of the journey.

I think it is for me.

God speed as you travel. I hope you find all the answers you're looking for and more!

~CHRIS BUTLER

BIBLIOGRAPHY

Arrien, Angeles. *The Tarot Handbook*. London, UK: Diamond Books, 1995.

Boyer, Janet. *The Back in Time Tarot Book*. Charlottesville, VA: Hampton Roads Publishing, 2008.

Bursten, Lee. *Universal Tarot of Marseille*. Torino, Italy: Lo Scarabeo, 2006.

Pollack, Rachel. *Complete Illustrated Guide to the Tarot*. London, UK: Harper Collins/Element, 2001.

Pollack, Rachel. *Seventy-Eight Degrees of Wisdom. A Book of Tarot*. London, UK: Harper Collins/Element,1997.

Sharman - Burke, Juliet. *Beginner's Guide to Tarot*. London, UK: Connections. 2001.

Warwick Smith, Kate. *The Tarot Court Cards*. Rochester, Vermont: Destiny Books. 2003.

MY ONLY REGRET about being gay is that I repressed it for so long. I surrendered my youth to the people I feared when I could have been out there loving someone. Don't make that mistake yourself. Life's too damn short.

~ARMISTEAD MAUPIN

Christopher Butler is an author, artist, and Tarot reader from the North West of England. He discovered the Tarot at the age of thirteen through watching a James Bond movie. His fascination for the cards has stayed with him for over thirty years, inspiring him to create several decks of his own along the way.

Chris received his first professional commission at the age of seventeen when *Space Voyager* magazine hired him to illustrate three interviews with cast members from the cult science fiction series *Doctor Who*. His first published Tarot deck was the *Quantum Tarot*, created in conjunction with author Kay Stopforth. A new version of this deck, *Quantum Tarot 2.0* is published by Lo Scarabeo.

Chris holds a Bachelor of Divinity degree from Heythrop College, University of London. He continues to work as an artist but now works as a professional Tarot reader as well. He lives in Liverpool, U.K.

For more information, visit Christopher's art website at: www.butlerart.co.uk and his Tarot reading website at: **www.Tarotinliverpool.com.**

Notes

Notes

Schiffer Books are available at special discounts for bulk purchases for sales promotions or premiums. Special editions, including personalized covers, corporate imprints, and excerpts can be created in large quantities for special needs. For more information contact the publisher:

Published by Schiffer Publishing, Ltd.
4880 Lower Valley Road
Atglen, PA 19310
Phone: (610) 593-1777; Fax: (610) 593-2002
E-mail: Info@schifferbooks.com

For the largest selection of fine reference books on this and related subjects, please visit our website at
www.schifferbooks.com
We are always looking for people to write books on new and related subjects. If you have an idea for a book, please contact us at
proposals@schifferbooks.com

This book may be purchased from the publisher.
Please try your bookstore first.
You may write for a free catalog.

In Europe, Schiffer books are distributed by
Bushwood Books
6 Marksbury Ave.
Kew Gardens
Surrey TW9 4JF England
Phone: 44 (0) 20 8392 8585; Fax: 44 (0) 20 8392 9876
E-mail: info@bushwoodbooks.co.uk
Website: www.bushwoodbooks.co.uk